Buy *Even* Lower

THE REGULAR PEOPLE'S GUIDE TO REAL ESTATE RICHES

Scott Frank

Andy Heller

Regular Riches®

KAPLAN PUBLISHING

President, Kaplan Publishing: Roy Lipner
Vice President and Publisher: Maureen McMahon
Acquisitions Editor: Victoria Smith
Director of Production: Daniel Frey
Production Editor: Caitlin Ostrow
Interior Design: Lucy Jenkins
Typesetter: Ellen Gurak

©2006 by Scott Frank and Andy Heller

Published by Kaplan Publishing, a division of Kaplan, Inc.

Printed in the United States of America

06 07 08 10 9 8 7 6 5 4 3 2 1

Library of Congress Cataloging-in-Publication Data

Frank, Scott (Scott M.)
   Buy even lower : the regular people's guide to real estate riches /
Scott Frank and Andy Heller.
      p. cm.
   ISBN-13: 978-1-4195-3574-1
   ISBN-10: 1-4195-3574-9
   1. Real estate investment--United States.   I. Heller, Andy. II. Title.
HD255.F665 2006
332.63'24--dc22   2006016184

Kaplan Publishing books are available at special quantity discounts to use for sales promotions, employee premiums, or educational purposes. Please call our Special Sales Department to order or for more information at 800-621-9621 ext. 4444, e-mail kaplanpubsales@kaplan.com, or write to Kaplan Publishing, 30 South Wacker Drive, Suite 2500, Chicago, IL 60606-7481.

SCOTT'S DEDICATION

This book is dedicated to my family. We've enjoyed a lot of great times and have been through some tough ones together. However, through it all, your unconditional love has made and continues to make life wonderful.

Marie, you are always by my side to support and encourage me, and you are a wonderful mother, wife, daughter, and sister. Dennis, Danielle, David, and Diana, you are truly gifts from God. You continue to keep life in perspective and make it so much fun.

To my dad (Denny), mom (Ellen), grandparents (Lucille, Melvin, Ella, and Oscar), and my stepfather (Barry), thanks for laying such a strong foundation regarding the significance and importance of family.

Brian and Marcy, you have been with me since I was just a little guy, and we have truly shared a lot together, including birthdays, weddings, childbirths, holiday celebrations, and Dunwoody.

Finally, Whitney, Addison, Olivia, Austin, Mike, Dylan, Jack, Caroline, Bonnie, Tom, Troy, Pauline, Leonora, Ginger, Seth, Cody, Maya, Moshe, Mala, Tamar, Daphna, Shua, Brad, Ellen, Adam, David, Sarah, Evelyn, Joe, Patty, Freddie, Jeffrey, Justin, Michael, Elizabeth, Alex, and Molly, you all continue to play an important role in making our family special.

You all have been there for me, and I hope to always be there for you. I'm blessed to have you in my life. I look forward to many more wonderful times together.

I also want to thank Andy for everything he's done for me and my family over the years. We've been through a lot together. You're a special person and I'm blessed to have you as a friend and business partner. Thanks for everything!

ANDY'S DEDICATION

I wish to dedicate this book to my family. To my new family, Stephany and Lily Rose, a special thanks for reminding me of the importance of balance in life. You are both beautiful flowers in my eyes. Stephany, I can always count on you to remind me that working hard all the time means little if you don't take the time to appreciate what's right in front of you and be reminded of what all the hard work is for. Don't ever let up on me.

To my mother, Barbara, and sister, Carrie. You have both been so supportive of all of my efforts for so many years, and especially during my early years. Thank you.

To the Starkmans, Nemoys, and Liebels in Canada. There may be a lot of geographic distance between us, but years after we emigrated to the United States, I'm happy to see that is the only distance between us.

To my dear father, Dr. E. Maurice Heller, who passed away in 1999. I watched and learned from you for so many years as you dedicated your professional and social life to charity and helping others. I always strive to live up to this wonderful example you gave me. We miss you more than words can express.

I wish to acknowledge a handful of people who have had a positive impact on my professional development. In my early years, Sidney Colen took interest in an energetic young kid and was generous in sharing his time and outlook on business with me. Don Fullilove, Juerg Bandle, and Peter Ulber have all left me with lessons too numerous to list.

Last, I wish to thank my dear friend and real estate partner, Scott. It has been a pleasure and privilege being your real estate partner and friend.

C *ontents*

FINALLY, A REGULAR PEOPLE'S BOOK FOR BUYING DISCOUNT REAL ESTATE

In 2003, we published our first book: *Buy Low, Rent Smart, and Sell High: Real Estate Investing for the Long Run*. This book details our unique investment strategy, a system that took us many years to develop. While we were confident we had something special to share, we weren't sure how our book and strategy would be received.

That's why, for first-time authors, we've been completely overwhelmed with the kudos from *Fortune, RealEstate Magazine, Publishers Weekly, The Working Investor, Black Enterprise,* columnists Bob Bruss and Ilyce Glink, and many others. We've been humbled by the countless thank-you notes and other forms of appreciation received from people who have read our book and used our strategy.

We've also been excited to receive a significant number of inquiries about buying real estate at a discount—what we call Buying Low. Requests have come through our seminars, speaking engagements, calls into radio interviews, and our Web site, *www.RegularRiches.com*. As a result, we recognize the need for a comprehensive and easy-to-read book to help "regular people" buy real estate at a discount and obtain maximum results from their efforts.

Who are these regular people? Those who currently invest (or are thinking about investing) in real estate on a part-time basis; those who haven't gone to a university to be formally educated on real estate investing; and those investors who are simply looking for ways to improve their methods. People exactly like us! Although we've been investing in real estate for many years, we consider ourselves regular people because we continue to invest on a part-time basis, we haven't been formally educated in real estate, and we're always looking for ways to improve.

In *Buy Even Lower: The Regular People's Guide to Real Estate Riches,* you'll read about the most prevalent approaches to Buy Even Lower. You'll learn about the process of buying low from start to finish, so you can apply your investment approach to consistently buy just about any type of real estate at a discount. In addition, you'll find helpful examples and strategies that are presented in an easy-to-understand format.

After you read this book, don't hesitate to go to our Web site, *www.RegularRiches.com,* with your questions and thoughts or to simply find additional educational information. We look forward to hearing from you.

We again give Barbara McNichol a special thanks for editing this book for us. In her own special way, she continues to transform our words into a much easier book to read. Thanks also to her assistant editor, Patrice Rhoades-Baum.

We also owe a special thanks to the Kaplan (still to us, the Dearborn) publishing team. We continue to be especially grateful to Mary B. Good for taking a chance on us, first-time writers, when we published our first book and for encouraging us now to write our second book and for then reviewing and editing it.

We also appreciate all the efforts and fine work of Maureen McMahon, Victoria Smith, Leslie Banks, Al Martin, and the rest of the Kaplan Publishing team.

Although the list is too long to mention everyone, we also want to give a special thanks to all the great people we've worked with over the years on our real estate team. Thank you Bernard and Deborah Newson, Charles and Lisa Chandler, Bonnie Gergens, Andy Shuping, Jay Lazega, Michael Warner, Al Stewart, Mike Barry, Jerome Rhodes, Bob Hodge, Ruthann Davies, Sheree Berk, Eddie Scott, Erin Lampe, Debbie Digby, Tim Sherrer, Susan Helms, Vicki Petty, James Burgin, Jon Ward, Chris McDonald, Brandwithin, Georgia Real Estate Investment Association (GAREIA), Karen Yapp, The Learning Annex, Samantha Del Canto, Learning Annex Toronto, Liz Walker, Hudson Valley REIA, Curt Darragh, PREIG of Canada, Navtaj Chandhoke, Big Apple REIA, Al Johnson, BAWB, Mike Morrongiello, NWB, Mike Sarwari, Las Vegas Magic, Luis Urquiaga, and Ken Walker.

YOUR REAL ESTATE ROAD TO RICHES

Because you're reading this book, we assume you've thought about getting rich with real estate. After all, real estate has developed a reputation for being a "road to riches." What are the potential riches and how do you travel this road?

To many, riches means millions of dollars. To some, it means financial freedom. To others, it simply means earning enough money to provide adequately for their families and live a comfortable retirement.

To us, riches means living a full and wonderful life. We want to be able to spend quality time with people we love, provide our families with what they need, live a comfortable lifestyle, help others in need, and enjoy the wonders that life has to offer. We refer to our definition of riches as *Regular Riches*® and believe most of you seek the same kind of riches we do.

Yes, having millions of dollars can help you achieve Regular Riches. However, the pursuit of millions can also hurt your chances of achieving Regular Riches because this wealth depends on having both money and time.

If you had an infinite amount of time, you would be able to spend as much time as you wanted with your family and friends and on other activities you enjoy or dream of doing. You would also have enough time to make the money needed for everything associated with these riches. However, you don't have unlimited time.

In fact, the time and money needed to meet your Regular Riches dreams are often at odds with the dreams themselves. Family expenses, annual vacation, college tuition, and new cars all cost money. Because you want your dreams to come true, you put in more hours on the job. However, working more takes time away from family, friends, and activities you enjoy. This situation also potentially takes away from your ability to make your immediate dreams come true; plus, working more doesn't guarantee you will realize your Regular Riches in the long run. Why? Because most jobs won't provide the long-term financial resources you'll need. Many jobs simply don't pay enough, and they may not even last in today's downsizing economy.

Additionally, many people who invest in stocks and bonds are betting on investments they do not fully understand. Stocks and bonds yield anything but a sure thing. Certificates of deposit and money market accounts are usually a safe bet but they often take a very long time to return a big payoff.

There are many ways to make better use of your time and money—and real estate investing is one of them. The key is *knowledge*. The best news is that you can acquire the knowledge you need to be a successful real estate investor without significant difficulty—no formal college or graduate education required.

Why Real Estate Investing?

How does real estate investing better position you to achieve Regular Riches dreams than some other methods? Let's take a look.

First, there's the return on your *time* component. Done properly, the hourly return on your real estate investments should be substantially larger than most hourly or salaried jobs yield. For example, if your job pays $25 an hour, you'd make $1,000 a week when you work a 40-hour week. If you work 20 hours of overtime, you may get paid time and a half, bringing your pay up to $1,750 a week. If you get paid a salary of $2,000 a week, you'll probably receive $2,000 whether you work 40, 50, or 60 hours.

On the other hand, many real estate investors are able to spend the same 40 hours (possibly spread out over a three-month or four-month period) and turn this time investment into tens of thousands of dollars (and sometimes hundreds of thousands of dollars). We show you this in the next chapter. Simply put, real estate investing often requires significantly less time than other wealth-building methods. Plus, real estate investors gain the flexibility for the Regular Riches that only having extra hours can "buy": time with family and friends to do enjoyable activities.

Next, let's look at the return on *money* component. Handled properly, the money you invest in real estate should have substantially lower risks and higher returns than standard stocks, bonds, certificates of deposits, and other investing vehicles. High-performing stock and even mutual fund investments are difficult to select (even for the trained investment professional). Also, for each stock that goes up 20 percent in a year, many others lose 20 percent of their value during the same period.

Additionally, if the stock market returns an average of 10 percent, most people are ecstatic. Good bonds and certificates of deposit usually grow much more slowly. On the other hand, many real estate investors consistently realize more than 10 percent return on their investment. In addition, stocks, bonds, and certificates of deposit usually require paying full price for the asset before you can gain a return. However, if you buy real estate, you often need to pay only 10 to 20 percent of the total value of the asset to receive a significant return.

This form of investing is proven. It's not a recent fad. Just as important, the knowledge you need to be a successful real estate investor is something most people can acquire without a formal education. Successful real estate investors read books like this one, invest in home study materials, attend seminars, and work with mentors to develop the knowledge they need. The sooner you gain the knowledge to invest in real estate properly, the sooner you will have more time and money to make your Regular Riches dreams come true.

Example: **S**tock versus **R**eal **E**state **I**nvestment

If a stock sells for $100, you will pay $100,000 cash to purchase 1,000 shares. If the stock goes up $10, then you make $10,000 ($10 × 1,000 shares). This equates to a 10 percent return on investment ($10,000 profit divided by your $100,000 total investment). By comparison, if you buy a house that sells for $100,000, you may need to pay only $10,000 cash to own it (a 10 percent down payment). If you sell it for $10,000 more than you paid for it ($110,000), you earn $10,000—and your return is 100 percent. Why the big difference? You didn't need to have $100,000 on hand to buy the real estate investment as you did for the stock investment. You simply leveraged the bank's money in the form of a loan to obtain your profits. (By the way, the interest on the real estate loan, unlike for most loans, is tax deductible.) In sum, real estate often requires significantly less money to get started while giving you a substantially higher return than many other wealth-building methods.

Key Principle: Buy Low

What do you need to know to ensure you're investing in real estate properly? Most successful investors tell you it comes down to *buying at a low price.* This principle may seem obvious. After all, investors in all areas often talk about buying low and selling high. However, when buying stocks and bonds, it's often difficult to determine whether you're actually buying low. However, with real estate, buying low consistently is usually much easier to verify and quantify at the time of purchase.

Additionally, to *Buy Even Lower* is about *more than just saving money* on your real estate investment. This book will also show you how to *save time and energy* as you proceed through the process.

In this book, we've taken approximately 40 years of our combined real estate investing experience and made learning about buying low easy for you. *Buy Even Lower* gives you a straightforward, comprehensive, and proven system for purchasing real estate *and* earning a profit.

We've used the steps outlined in this book to help make our Regular Riches dreams come true and so have many other successful investors. Our hope is that, by following our system, you can make your Regular Riches dreams come true, too.

1

BECOMING A MILLIONAIRE

Meet Jack and Jill. They are both regular, everyday people who are interested in investing their money in real estate. Jack and Jill are both smart, industrious, and hardworking individuals who are eager to get started on their first real estate transaction. As you'll see, one of them takes the appropriate steps to achieve a successful investment, but the other does not.

JACK'S "THOUSANDAIRE" STORY

Jack decides that he's going to find a good property, buy it at a discount, and determine whether to sell or rent it depending on the property's attributes. He has heard a lot about Lake RegularRiches, which is about 30 minutes from his house. He hears the properties are "hot" in this nice lake community. Jack believes this is a perfect place for an investor to make good money, and indeed it is, or it *could be*.

Jack gets on the Internet and immediately finds a condominium that is selling for less than the others. While the other two-bedroom, two-bathroom condos are selling for $200,000 or more, this one is listed for just $160,000.

He immediately calls the listing agent who tells him that an older couple had owned it for about 20 years, and they both recently passed away. The condo was just listed earlier today, and the owners' children have priced it to sell quickly. He is told that it is right on the lake, and it's in good condition. The agent says he's had a lot of inquiries already and expects it to go fast. Jack and the agent agree to meet in one hour. The agent tells Jack that he's "lucky," as he is the first one to view the property.

As he walks the place, Jack loves what he sees. Yes, the carpet, kitchen, and bathrooms are a little dated (probably the original stuff) but everything seems to be functional and in overall good condition. He loves being the one to find this "substantially discounted" property first. He considers whether he has time to do a little more research and whether he'll lose the property if he comes in with an offer lower than the Asking Price. However, when the agent tells him that he has four more showings later in the day, Jack feels pressured to make a decision now to scoop up this deal. He's certain that this is a great deal, and he's not going to let someone else snatch it out from under him later in the day. He tells the agent he'll take it. The agent fills out a standard real estate sales contract, and Jack signs it. On the ride home, Jack can't stop thinking about his good fortune.

Jack closes on the property in 30 days and has decided to sell it immediately. The thought of being a landlord doesn't excite him, while the quick cash profit and nice boost to his bank account does. Immediately after the closing, Jack places For Sale ads in the local newspaper and on the Internet. His Asking Price is $200,000. The first week, Jack gets some calls and shows the property to a handful of perspective buyers. However, he gets no offers.

The second week, he gets equally as many calls and showings. He also finally gets his first offer . . . $150,000. Jack is taken aback. Is this a joke? Should he counteroffer at $195,000? He decides not to take it seriously and doesn't respond.

The third week is essentially a repeat of week two. He gets another offer for $150,000. Jack is perplexed. He decides to ask this buyer her rationale. What he hears *surprises him*. He's told that most of the properties in the complex have been significantly updated, while his condominium is not. *Jack didn't know this*. He's also told that the missing view of the lake, since the condo was on the first floor, made the value of the property less than on higher floors in the complex. *Jack hadn't considered this*. Finally, he's told that being situated near the complex dumpster also impacts the value. *Jack hadn't even noticed this*.

Jack considers all this information. Sure, the condo may not be as perfect as all the others, but it can't be too far off. All he needs is one good buyer. He decides to reduce the Asking Price 5 percent to $190,000. He will now be able to show buyers that he understands the negative attributes, and he'll still clear a nice profit. Another few weeks go by without an offer. The marketing, utilities, and mortgage payments are now on the verge of making a real impact on his profits. Therefore, he decides to contact an expert for some help . . . a licensed real estate agent.

The real estate agent tells him that with the proper marketing, he can probably get close to $185,000. However, he'll have to spend about $8,000 to update the place because most people don't want to be hassled with fixer-uppers. Jack signs on with the agent and hires a contractor. The place is ready for showing within a month.

Good news for Jack. The real estate agent brings him an offer for $185,000 within days of putting the condo back on the market. He immediately signs the contract, and the property is sold 30 days later.

Jack's very happy to have the property sold. However, he's not nearly as happy about his profits. After a significant amount of time dealing with the property, and after paying for the improvements and real estate agent commission, he has cleared only $1,900. Jack has now become very disillusioned with real estate investing and decides there must be better ways for him to make good money.

Jack's Profits from the Condo Sale	
Sales price	$185,000
6% real estate commission	(11,100)
Carpet, kitchen, and bathroom updates	(8,000)
Utilities, marketing, mortgage payments	(4,000)
Purchase price	(160,000)
Jack's profit	$1,900

Because Jack didn't do his research and didn't know the appropriate steps to take to ensure a profitable transaction, he is discouraged by the results and decides that real estate investing is not for him.

JILL'S "MILLIONAIRE" STORY

While Jack has become frustrated with real estate investing, Jill has gradually become more and more confident. Before she got started, she wisely read our book *Buy Even Lower*. She then began to use the Six Golden Keys that we define below to find her first investment property.

GOLDEN KEY 1—Determine Your Minimum Investor Discount

Jill assesses her personal situation to choose the investment strategy that will work best for her. She has learned about the three primary strategies and their pros and cons described for Golden Key 1. Jill isn't sure she will have a lot of time to consistently devote to real estate property management. Therefore, she chooses the buy at a discount and quick sell strategy, also known as "buying and flipping." As outlined for Golden Key 1, Jill determines that her *minimum investor discount* for buying and flipping this property will be *20 percent.*

GOLDEN KEY 2—Know What Good Properties Look Like

Jill now needs to determine what type of property will be good for her. With her limited real estate experience and goal to start now, she has learned from the book that residential properties will probably work better for her than commercial ones. Jill also has learned about the variety of residential options, and how to select the best one for the situation. Using some of the tips for Golden Key 2, she learns that one of the best markets for buyers and sellers currently is *two-bedroom, two-bathroom properties in the lake communities within 30 minutes from her home.* Since Jill wants to buy and flip properties, she then decides that these will be the type of properties she will target.

GOLDEN KEY 3—Find Good Properties

Jill next considers the best ways to find these properties. For Golden Key 3, she has learned that there are many ways to choose from. Again, based on her limited amount of time, she chooses to *contact banks to buy foreclosed properties, also known as postforeclosures.*

She uses the techniques she has learned to find these properties at three different banks. Several look promising. One of them is a two-bedroom, two-bathroom condominium on the first floor of a 20-story complex in a community called Lake RegularRiches. The bank has just put it on the market and is asking $160,000.

GOLDEN KEY 4—Calculate Maximum Purchase Prices

Jill knows she needs to calculate the most she should pay for this condo. Golden Key 4 gave her the formula for this, the Maximum Purchase Price. She reminds herself that the formula is *critical* to ensure that the purchase is worth her while. Jill does a little research and finds out that most of the two-bedroom, two-bathroom condos are selling for $200,000 or more. She contacts the bank's real estate agent to set up a time the next day to see it. *Jill is excited.*

As Jill heads off to meet the bank's agent at the property, she is ready to take notes on it. She gets there early to walk the outside. She notices that the lake view for the first floor condos is obstructed by trees and her target condo is located near the complex's dumpster. She notes these negative attributes on her pad for future use. *Jill gets more excited.*

Jill then walks the condo with the agent. She learns that an older couple had owned the condo for about 20 years. When they passed away, their only child inherited it and took out a 95 percent loan against it. Within a year, he had defaulted on the loan, and the bank had foreclosed on the property. As she views the interior, Jill likes what she sees. The place is in good condition. However, the carpet, kitchen, and bathrooms are outdated. *Jill gets even more excited.*

This is exactly the type of "good property" she was targeting. The condo in this hot community meets her two-bedroom, two-bathroom criteria. Additionally, it has a variety of negatives that will probably turn most buyers off. For this reason, she knows the bank may have a hard time selling it. *This could be the perfect property to "buy even lower."*

By following the formula below, Jill is now ready to determine the *Maximum Purchase Price* she should pay to make an appropriate investor profit.

She knows the Fair Market Value (FMV) of most of the other units in the complex is $200,000. However, she is very observant and notices the unit next door sold last month for $185,000 and has some similar negative attributes (bad view and nearby dumpster). Jill has a reputable contractor take a look at the property for her, and she estimates the costs to upgrade it at $8,000. She now has her Repairs and Improvement Costs (R&I).

Next, she estimates all the Other Costs (OC) that she will need to spend to get the property bought and sold. These costs include closing costs, loan finance costs, marketing costs, utility costs, and even a 6 percent real estate commission of $11,100 (she plans to use an agent to minimize her time and, hopefully, maximize her profit). Jill estimates that it will take a few months to fix and sell and that the Other Costs are $15,000.

Finally, Jill estimates the Total Investor Discount (TID) she needs to make a profit by determining the Total Investor Discount Percentage and multiplying it by the Fair Market Value. To determine the percentage, she uses the Minimum Investor Discount of 20 percent that she determined at Golden Key 1 (further described in Chapter 2), based on the investment strategy she is using (Buy and Flip). She then adds 8 percent more for the bad view and dumpster negative property attributes, as well as the hassle (time and energy) for updating the property. Jill arrives at a 28 percent Total Investor Discount Percentage and multiplies this by the Fair Market Value of $185,000 to arrive at a Total Investor Discount of $51,800.

Jill now knows that, as a Buy and Flip investor, the most she should pay for the property, the *Maximum Purchase Price*, is $110,200.

Jill knows this is a lot less than the $160,000 that the bank is asking. However, she also knows that the bank might just have some difficulty selling this property. As she has learned in *Buy*

Jill's Maximum Purchase Price for Condo	
Fair Market Value	$185,000
Less: Repairs and Improvement Costs	(8,000)
Less: Other Costs	(15,000)
Less: Total Investor Discount	(51,800)
Maximum Purchase Price	$110,200

Even Lower, most buyers do not like fixer-uppers. Also, it is now October and she knows that the bank is entering the slowest real estate sales period of the year.

GOLDEN KEY 5—Make Solid Offers

Jill now sets out to put a solid offer together. For Golden Key 5, she remembers to almost never come in with an initial offer price equal to the Maximum Purchase Price. She will need ample room to negotiate. Using the techniques in the book, she decides on an Initial Offer Price of $100,000. Jill runs this potential offer through a few of the tests in the book, and she believes it passes. She then fills in the blanks on the real estate purchase contract from the book (which has been reviewed and modified by a local real estate attorney to conform to her local laws).

Jill then uses the book's guidelines to craft a cover letter explaining her rationale for the substantially discounted offer. *She summarizes the pluses and minuses of the property, and then walks the seller through the calculations behind her $100,000 initial offer price.*

She is a little bit nervous about making her first real estate investment offer. However, *Jill is very excited and anxious to take this step.*

Jill calls up the agent and they meet. She talks the agent through the analysis in the cover letter and then hands it to her with the signed contract and earnest money.

After a couple of days, Jill is still waiting for a response from the bank. She knows that patience might play a very big role in this negotiation. That evening, she finally receives a call from the agent. The bank has countered her offer at $150,000.

GOLDEN KEY 6—Negotiate Like a Chess Master

That night Jill rereads the section in the book on negotiating. For Golden Key 6, she is reminded about *not coming up on her offer too quickly, being patient, and not exceeding her Maximum Purchase Price*. Yes, Jill and the bank are currently $50,000 apart on the offers, and about $40,000 apart from her Maximum Purchase Price of $110,200. However, she knows that if she plays it right, she could end up buying this property at the appropriate price. She decides to look at some other properties that meet her criteria and to use the *Lay Low strategy* from the book over the coming month.

The next month, she contacts the agent to see if the property is still available and finds that it is. She then spends that evening considering her next move. Again, she uses some of the techniques from the book. She decides to increase her offer price to $105,000. Jill *marks through and handwrites the new date and offer price* on the contract and cover letter, and writes in an explanation of her counteroffer on the cover letter. The next day, she meets the agent, walks her through the rationale behind the counteroffer, and hands it to her.

Later that day, she hears from the agent. The bank has decided to come down to $140,000. Jill considers the current situation and decides to continue looking at other properties and lay low again.

A month later, Jill checks on the property. It is still on the market. She then faxes the agent a bumped up offer of $110,000. Jill uses the same cover letter as last time. Again, she repeats the process from her last offer, including simply marking through the old date and offer price and handwriting the new one plus a short note. She's now just $200 away from her Maximum Purchase Price.

The next day, the agent calls to tell her the bank is willing to accept $130,000. She realizes they're getting closer to her Maximum Purchase Price of $110,200, but the two sides are still almost $20,000 apart.

Jill then makes a conscious decision to lay low again and wait another month before following up with the bank. She knows the property could be sold by then, but she is not going to pay too much for it.

One month later, Jill checks the Internet for the listing. She is a little surprised to see it still listed at $160,000, especially when she knew the bank was willing to accept $130,000. This might explain why the property is still on the market. The book has prepared her for this, too. Jill then meets the agent again with her revised offer of $110,200, talks her through it, and hands her the same old contract and cover letter with the same old mark-throughs and a new date and offer price. She remembers how the book has taught her about the psychological impact such a letter may have many months into a negotiation.

The next day the agent calls her and says, "The bank will accept $120,000." She is now so close, she can taste her first investment purchase. Jill just has to figure out a way to bridge the final $9,800 gap.

She waits another month, and the property is still on the market. Following the strategies from the book, Jill meets the agent again and hands her the previous offer with the new date and price, as well as the words *"best and final offer"* on the cover letter. She explains that this is simply the highest she can go. Jill knows that it might not be accepted, but she also knows that this is the right time to make this kind of offer. Hopefully, *the bank will appreciate her professionalism and consistency over the last few months and bite on this offer . . . and they do.*

Thirty days later, Jill is the proud owner of her first real estate investment property. She has lined up a contractor and real estate agent prior to closing, and the condo is updated and on the market just a couple weeks after closing. Jill's Asking Price is $185,000, and she receives an offer for the condo the first week it is listed. Thirty days later, Jill's first investment property had been sold. *Jill is thrilled. She has cleared $53,700, and is eager to buy and sell more real estate.*

Jill's Profits from Condo Sale	
Sales price	$185,000
6% real estate commission	(11,100)
Carpet, kitchen, bathroom updates	(8,000)
Utilities, marketing, mortgage payments	(2,000)
Purchase price	(110,200)
Jill's profits	$53,700

THEIR HAPPY AND NOT-SO-HAPPY ENDINGS

As you'll notice, Jack and Jill sold their equivalent properties for exactly the same price, and both paid the same real estate commission and update costs. However, Jill was following a specific investment strategy early on. She spent about half the amount of time selling the property and saved money on utilities, marketing, and mortgage costs. Most important, because Jill used the Six Golden Keys from *Buy Even Lower,* she was able to generate profits of $53,700 from this single property, while Jack only generated $1,900 from the equivalent property.

Jack never invested in real estate again, instead choosing to dabble in stocks and bonds. He never made much money doing this, and remained a "thousandaire." Jill on the other hand, continued investing in real estate. Ten years later, she was a "millionaire."

In our many years of real estate investing, we know both of these stories all too well. Yes, the particular names of the characters, as well as the actual real estate purchase details, vary, sometimes substantially. However, the general themes do not. The reality is that there are still many, many people buying investment real estate just like Jack. At the same time, there are a lot fewer people doing it successfully—like Jill.

We have purchased investment real estate much like Jill many times. More specifically, *we've used the Six Golden Keys to Buy Even Lower, grow our wealth, and achieve Regular Riches*. If you use the Golden Keys, then you should be able to achieve them, too. We wish you the best on this journey along your "Road to Regular Riches."

2

GOLDEN KEY 1—DETERMINE YOUR MINIMUM TOTAL INVESTOR DISCOUNT

The Minimum Investor Discount Percentage is one of the most important aspects of real estate investing. However, it is also one that is often overlooked, especially by novice investors.

The Minimum Investor Discount is the smallest profit an investor should make on any real estate purchase. In other words, the Minimum Investor Discount represents the amount of money from the profits the investor will be able to put in the bank account after the property is purchased and then resold.

The Minimum Investor Discount assumes that a property is in mint condition and cost-free. In other words, whether it is a house, office building, or simply a piece of vacant land, the Minimum Investor Discount assumes that the investor will have no repair or improvement costs, no finance costs, no real estate commissions, and so on. If any additional costs will be incurred, they need to be considered for additional purchase price discounting because, again, the Minimum Investor Discount is the minimum profit that the investor should make on the real estate investment.

Some investors simply use a dollar amount, such as $25,000, $50,000, or $100,000. If they can find an investment property where they can make this type of money, then they go after it. Without a doubt, a Minimum Investor Discount of $25,000, not to mention $50,000 or $100,000, is very good money for most people, including us. However, there is one big problem with this strategy.

Investors who rely on flat dollar amounts for their Minimum Investor Discount are ignoring an important factor—risk. More specifically, an investor who buys a $100,000 house for $50,000 is taking a lot less risk than an investor who buys a $500,000 house for $450,000. Both received a $50,000 discount. However, if something goes wrong with the $100,000 property (structural problems, neighborhood values decrease, etc.), that investor is likely only to lose thousands, maybe many thousands, or even tens of thousands of dollars. On the other hand, if the investor of the $500,000 property runs into similar problems, he or she is easily at risk of losing tens of thousands, maybe many tens of thousands, or even hundreds of thousands of dollars.

Accordingly, investors who buy the same price properties every time may be able to determine a Minimum Investor Discount dollar amount that works for them every time. However, since most investors vary their purchase prices (if not initially, generally most long-term investors vary over time) and real estate prices tend to go up (almost all of the time, though it may take some time), we recommend that you use a percentage instead of a flat dollar amount. We call this the *Minimum Investor Discount Percentage (MID%)*.

Now, it would sure be nice if every investor could buy properties with a MID% of 50 percent or even 33 percent. If an investor could do this consistently, his or her real estate investing fortunes would just about be guaranteed.

However, in the real world, deals like this are rare. Additionally, those properties that are selling at such a discount are often in very bad neighborhoods, are in very poor condition, or have other significant problems. Therefore, they still might not be a good buy. With this being said, the smaller the MID%, the larger the pool of possible properties to purchase.

Accordingly, if an investor's MID% is 0 percent (no discount), then just about every property on the market is a possibility. Unfortunately, obtaining Regular Riches from these types of real estate purchases becomes a lot harder.

With all of this in mind, most investors buy properties with a discount of 5 to 30 percent. To determine your MID%, the primary factor will be your selected *investment strategy*. When you've chosen this, you will have a MID% range to choose from. Your decision to select at or near the bottom of the range, such as 5 percent, versus at or near the top of the range, such as 30 percent, will be dependent on how much money, time, and energy you choose to spend looking for properties. Again, the smaller the MID%, the more investment real estate you will have to choose from, and the easier it will be for you to find properties to Buy Even Lower. On the other hand, the higher the MID%, the smaller your pool of potential properties becomes, and the harder it will be to find good properties to purchase.

DIFFERENT STRATEGIES REQUIRE DIFFERENT DISCOUNTS

Each real estate investment strategy requires different considerations for buying property. Each has different short-, intermediate-, and long-term profit horizons as well as different risks and up-front requirements of money, time, and energy.

There are three primary investment strategies, with most other strategies being variations of these three. The first is the *Buy and Flip strategy*, which means the investor buys the property at a significant discount and quickly puts it up for sale. The second is the *Buy and Hold strategy*, which means the investor buys the property and elects to rent it or let it sit with no intention of selling it in the foreseeable future. The third is the *Buy and Lease/Purchase strategy,* which means the investor purchases the property and contracts with a tenant in a rent-to-own relationship.

Because of the different profit time horizons, risks, and costs (money, time, and energy), we suggest choosing an investment strategy that meets *your personal situation.* Some investors assume they can make this decision after the purchase of the investment property is complete. However, as mentioned above, because each investment strategy requires a different MID% for the strategy to deliver the promised profits, it's best to choose your investment strategy early in the Buy Even Lower process. If you don't, you risk investing money, time, and energy looking at properties that you should never purchase. You may also end up paying too much for properties and, possibly, even losing money on these transactions.

The following will show you how the MID% works with the different investment strategies. We'll also walk you through the trade-offs in investor time horizons, risks, money, energy, and more.

DISCOUNT FOR BUY AND FLIP STRATEGY

Generally, the Buy and Flip strategy is about making the quick buck. Buy a property at a discount, get it ready for marketing, and sell it for short-term gain. Your profits are the difference between the sales price and the purchase price, less all related costs including repair costs, holding costs, and real estate commissions.

The Buy and Flip strategy almost always requires buying very low—with Minimum Investor Discounts of 20 to 30 percent, or more. It also usually involves trying to sell at top dollar. Often, it involves getting the property cleaned up, repaired, and improved as quickly as possible because every extra day the investor retains ownership in the property means the holding costs (utilities, advertising, mortgage payments, etc.) go up.

This strategy has one attribute that's particularly attractive to many investors: The time horizon to realize profit for each property is relatively short, especially compared to the other two strategies. Investors can then use these profits to buy more properties and potentially grow their wealth faster than with the other two strategies.

However, it has some drawbacks. For one, as discussed above, the pool of properties with huge discounts is usually very small. Therefore, the time between purchases may be lengthy and the money, time, and effort expended to find deeply discounted properties may be much higher than with the other two strategies.

Also, because time isn't on your side when selling, this strategy carries the biggest risk. Holding costs increase every day the investor owns the property. That means the longer it takes to sell the property, the more the investor's profits are degraded. The investor may even feel pushed to discount the property or involve a costly real estate agent, which would further eat into profits. Because of the quick-sell time pressures, this strategy can be stressful.

Many investors have used the Buy and Flip strategy with great success. However, if you're going to utilize this strategy, you need to understand it well. In Chapter 1, Jill did and Jack did not.

DISCOUNT FOR BUY AND HOLD STRATEGY

This strategy is generally about finding properties with good rental or appreciation potential. Most investors who use this model buy houses, condominiums, multifamily properties (duplexes, triplexes, quadplexes, apartment buildings), or commercial real estate (office buildings, strip centers). Some investors buy undeveloped land, build on it, and rent out the buildings. These landlord investors usually collect monthly rents, apply a portion to pay down the loan each month, and keep the difference as monthly profit. Eventually, they sell this real estate, hoping to realize even more profits from the property's appreciation.

On the other hand, some investors choose to simply buy and sit on property, and then wait for it to appreciate. This type of investor often buys large tracts of property in rural areas or purchases smaller pieces of land in suburban or urban communities. Regardless of the approach, the investor will usually have to pay some money out of pocket each year to pay tax bills (which can be significant, especially if the property appreciates nicely).

Unlike the Buy and Flip strategy, which is about fast, short-term profits, the Buy and Hold strategy is about slow, long-term profits. Accordingly, though the investor will likely be looking to buy properties at a discount, this is not a requirement. Many Buy and Hold investors rely on investor discounts as small as 5 to 10 percent. After all, most of these investors expect to make the majority of their profits from monthly rents, tax write-offs from being a landlord, paying down the loan with the tenants' money, and property appreciation over the long haul. Many Buy and Hold investors see the greatest upside 15 or 30 years into the future, when the typical loan is paid off. Some of these 30-year loan investors simply sell the paid-for property to fund their retirement years.

This strategy has two good characteristics. First, there is a relatively large pool of properties available to investors looking to buy at a Minimum Investor Discount of 5 to 10 percent (and a huge pool of properties available at no discount). Therefore, the investors using this strategy won't have a lot of trouble finding property to buy. Second, the relatively long investment-time horizon tends to be more stable, which allows investors to ride through good and bad economic times.

On the other hand, Buy and Hold investors must be patient with their profits and sometimes with their tenants. Unlike Buy and Flip investors who can potentially grow their profits fast and reinvest these earnings into more properties, Buy and Hold investors must acquire most of their cash from other sources to buy more properties. Additionally, because landlord investors plan to own their properties for a long time, they'll have to make additional money, time, and energy investments while owning their properties to repair, maintain, and rerent them. Finally, because these investments are long term, they carry risk that the community or neighborhood may depreciate in value by the time they're finally ready to sell.

DISCOUNT FOR BUY AND LEASE/PURCHASE STRATEGY

This strategy is our preferred real estate investment strategy. From our perspective, it encompasses the best qualities of the Buy and Flip and the Buy and Hold strategies, while minimizing many of their negative attributes. However, this strategy is primarily for investors looking to invest in properties that can be relatively easy to rent and sell to a tenant. That's why it works best with houses and can also be used with condominiums, town homes, and certain office buildings. However, it doesn't generally work well with apartment buildings, big commercial properties, or undeveloped land.

The profit-time horizon for this strategy is short term, intermediate term, and long term because, after being purchased by the investor, these properties are marketed as "rent to buy." For example, a homebuyer can answer the ad for lease/purchasing and buy it outright. When that happens, the investor generates a fast, short-term profit by flipping the home. Some lease/purchasers (rent-to-buy tenants) purchase in the intermediate term (within the first few years after the investor purchases the property) or in the long term, which makes it a long-term investment.

Because of these different scenarios, investors can tap into the five different profit sources described for the other two strategies. Specifically, they can gain access to the profits from buying at a Minimum Investor Discount, as well as collecting monthly rents, realizing property appreciation, obtaining tax write-offs from being a landlord, and paying down the loan with the lease/purchaser's money. This strategy also opens the door to a sixth profit source: option money, which is the fee the lease/purchaser pays to enter into a lease/purchase agreement. In our model, the fee may be applied to the purchase of the property but is forfeited if the lease/purchaser chooses not to buy.

As a result of these six diversified profit sources specific to the Buy and Lease/Purchase strategy, investors don't need to find properties at *deep* discounts, unlike with the Buy and Flip strategy. However, they do need a larger discount than Buy and Hold investors because the property could be resold quickly. Therefore, the rule of thumb we typically use for the Minimum Investor Discount is 10 to 20 percent. Most communities have a good supply of these properties discounted in this range, if you know where to find them (which we discuss for Golden Key 3).

Like the Buy and Flip investor, the Buy and Lease/Purchase investor from time to time receives short-term cash windfalls from the sales of their properties, which can be used to buy more. Plus, like the Buy and Hold investor, the Buy and Lease/Purchase investor doesn't have to make short-term bets on sales prices because the intermediate-term and long-term components of this strategy provide a safety net.

On the other hand, unlike the Buy and Flip strategy, the Buy and Lease/Purchase strategy usually turns the investor into a landlord (as in the Buy and Hold strategy). But using our model, the Buy and Lease/Purchase investor transfers all repair and maintenance obligations to the lease purchaser; this substantially reduces the likelihood of late-night calls and surprise costs associated with these properties. Because our model leverages a three-year lease/purchase agreement, the time, money, and headaches associated with re-leasing every year or two are substantially reduced. And because most lease/purchasers anticipate buying the property, they tend to pay their rent on time and take better care of the property than an average tenant does.

THE ROLE YOUR PERSONAL SITUATION PLAYS

Which investment strategy you select depends on your personal situation. In discussing this, we'll focus on typical key factors

Create Win-Win Lease/Purchase Agreements

Not all books and seminars on lease/purchases structure their agreements the same way we do. Our goal is to create a win-win situation to maximize our profits and minimize our time and energy. The win for the lease/purchasers is the fair rent and the locked-in sales price for the fair market value of the property at the time the lease/purchase is signed. In many cases, we're simply giving them up to three years to save enough money for a down payment and repair their credit, if necessary. Yes, they pay us a fee (the option money) for the right to lock in the sales price at the current fair market value. However, they can apply the option money (equivalent to the monthly rent payment) to the purchase of the property. By doing this, we attract people who are more likely to pay their rent on time and take good care of the property (and often improve it) because they expect to buy it.

With this agreement, we win by being able to transfer all repair and maintenance obligations to the lease/purchasers, and we don't often need to rerent the property for long periods of time (if ever). Plus, we receive a fair market rent payment and get cash windfalls every so often when the lease/purchasers buy the property. Although we might leave some money on the table when a property appreciates and is then bought by the lease/purchasers, we believe we more than make up for this with the money, time, and energy saved by having stable tenants and transferring the repair and maintenance obligations to them. This low-maintenance landlording frees up more money, time, and energy than normal landlording does so we can enjoy our Regular Riches (spending time with our family, friends, and other activities) and buy more properties.

that you and other real estate investors face: time, effort, stress, headaches, cash, and credit.

Time and Effort

Many investment gurus focus the content of their books and seminars on their strategy, assuming you have the time and effort to implement it. In our experience, even if you have the money and knowledge, a great real estate investment strategy is worthless when you don't have these components in your life. Start by realistically assessing the time and effort investment you can make, given the needs of your family, your full-time job, your hobbies, and anything else that might affect your real estate investing.

You may be thinking that you'll put in whatever time and effort is necessary to make your dreams come true for you and your family. You also may think: "For the right amount of money, my family won't miss my taking time away from them." You may even think, "If I can make big money from real estate investing, then my full-time job is irrelevant because I'll quit." Or you say, "Real estate investing will be a hobby, so I'll simply dip into my hobby-time bucket to do it." Perhaps you think you can forgo a few hours sleep each night, or you have other areas where you'd find time. Yet, because some real estate investment strategies take more time and effort than others (some significantly more), be realistic when you assess the amount of time and effort you'll have available.

For example, the Buy and Flip strategy often requires significant amounts of your time during the buying phase because you must find properties at a deep discount (often 25 percent or more). Because the pool of properties with this type of discount is usually small, you'll have to work extra hard and invest significant time and effort to find them. Once you buy a property, you'll actively look to sell it quickly. Therefore, the actual number of days and effort you have to spend on this property may be a lot less than for the Buy and Hold and Buy and Lease/Purchase investor.

On the other hand, the Buy and Hold strategy may take a little or a lot of time in the buying phase, depending on the amount of discount you require. Remember, you expect to make most of your profits from renting over the long haul and the appreciation when you eventually sell. You'd likely spend less time seeking Buy and Hold properties than seeking the others; in this case, getting a deep discount isn't as crucial as for the other strategies. However, since you're reading this book, you're probably at least thinking of buying properties at a discount. Assume you'd spend a fair amount of time on the buying phase if you use this strategy.

However, if you're a Buy and Hold investor, the real time and effort investment occurs after you purchase the property—especially if you get stuck with "nightmare" tenants. Even if you have good tenants, expect to spend more time and effort with the Buy and Hold strategy to deal with issues (repairs, maintenance, rerenting) while you own the property. Now, if you're simply a Buy and Hold investor who will sit on the property (for example, undeveloped land), then you may expend less time and effort on this strategy than on any other strategy.

The Buy and Lease/Purchase strategy usually requires less time to find and buy property than the Buy and Flip strategy because you don't have to find a property with huge discounts to make your profits. You make your profits from rents, option money, and the other profit sources. In addition, the Buy and Lease/Purchase strategy allows you to attract better-than-average tenants, transfer the repair and maintenance responsibilities to the lease/purchasers (your tenants), and sign a lease/purchase agreement for several years (often three). Therefore, the time and effort you spend on a property should be substantially less than that of the Buy and Hold investor.

Stress and Headaches

Obviously, most people don't want to invite stress and headaches into their lives. However, some people are better at dealing with stress and headaches than others. In fact, many who try to avoid problem situations always seem to be stressed out, while others who seem to thrive on problems rarely get stressed out. Be honest with yourself about this assessment, knowing that different investment strategies bring different levels of stress and headaches.

Let's first look at problems common to all three strategies. No matter which strategy you follow, you'll usually find yourself in the "clean, repair, and improvement phase" after you buy the property. Although every property doesn't require full-scale cleaning, repairs, and improvements, most require some, so be mentally prepared to deal with contractors who don't finish the project under budget or on time, and a variety of repair and improvement decisions.

With the Buy and Flip strategy come two primary causes of stress and headaches that are often more substantial than with the other two strategies. The first is having to find properties to buy at deep discounts (usually much deeper than with the other two strategies). Your profit is usually closely related to how much below market you pay for your properties. Chances are, you'd have to deal with an excessive amount of time, dead ends, and frustration to find properties with 25 percent or greater Minimum Investor Discounts.

However, investors typically feel the most stress during the sell phase of the Buy and Flip strategy. Because the profits are actually realized after the sale of the property, every day that goes by—and the property goes unsold—eats into your profits. First, unless you use a real estate agent (which will cut into your profits), you'll probably deal with multiple people interested in buying the property. Next, there's the stress of watching the holding costs increase each day (utilities, mortgage payments, advertising costs, etc.). Finally, you have to deal with the additional stress and headaches of deciding if and when to reduce the sales price or include a real estate agent (and lose a portion of the profit to the agent's commission) to help sell the property. Under the pressure of this stress, you also may feel compelled to deal with difficult buyers who may make unrealistic demands.

The good news for Buy and Flip investors is that, unlike the other two investment types, the duration of stress and headaches per property is usually short—often just a few months and rarely more than a year.

The Buy and Hold strategy has its own stress and headache factors from landlording. The first stress often occurs during the rental phase, in which you may have to show a property multiple times and hold multiple phone conversations with potential tenants. During this phase, you could feel additional stress if the property remains vacant for an extended period of time. The stress associated with the monthly holding costs grows with every month the property remains vacant and may lead to further stress—the decision to reduce the rent to get the property rented. The second cause of stress happens during the actual tenancy phase. With rental properties, landlords never know when something will require immediate repair or attention. Problems with plumbing, the furnace, or the air conditioner never seem to happen at a convenient time. For many investors, getting that call makes their blood pressure rise and their minds quickly dart from "Who should I call" to "How much will this cost?" to "Will I need to buy a new one?" If you're a Buy and Hold investor, you feel additional stress if you have problem tenants calling at strange hours or complaining about trivial problems. Additionally, the stress usually mounts when tenants don't pay their rent on time, forcing you to deal with costly and time-consuming evictions. While you may choose to hire a management company to deal with these problems (and stress), this expense will eat into your profit. Plus, the company may not manage the property as well as you would, which could lead to further profit reductions (the absentee owner scenario).

The Buy and Hold landlord investor usually experiences longer periods of stress and headaches than investors using the other strategies, directly related to owning the property longer. However, the amount of stress the Buy and Hold landlord feels during the rental and tenancy phases is usually less than the stress the Buy and Flip investor feels during the sell phase. Why? Because all the profits for the Buy and Hold investor don't rest on the purchase and sale of the property. On the other hand, compared to the Buy and Lease/Purchase investor, the Buy and Hold landlord investor usually has more stress during the rental and tenancy phases. Buy and Lease/Purchase investors tend to attract more stable tenants, are able to transfer the repair and maintenance obligations to the lease/purchaser, and often achieve longer tenancy periods.

Cash and Credit

Cash is the amount of money you have in your bank account, in your wallet, and under your mattress. *Credit* is the amount of money you can get a bank or other financial institution to lend you.

Many people put off real estate investing because they prefer not to risk their own money or they simply don't have the cash or credit necessary to buy a property. That's why the "no money down" gurus are making such a killing with their books and seminars. In our experience, these types of deals are few and far between. Therefore, having your own cash and credit available will play a big role in determining the investment strategy that's right for you.

> **Caution: Borrowing from Friends, Family, and Other Investors**
>
> When you consider your available cash and credit, be careful about factoring in funds from friends, family, and investors. When we give seminars, we often meet people who are extremely excited about getting into real estate investing but don't have the cash or credit to match their excitement and many end up with big problems. In our experience, borrowing funds from friends and family members is one of the best ways to begin a family feud or lose a valuable friend. If you're considering entering into a partnership, do so carefully. Many partnerships end up in a breakup over a disagreement. Thoroughly discuss your short-term and long-term goals and respective roles, then document the agreements you make.

When considering your credit, get a copy of your credit report and take time to understand it. Many financial institutions don't lend money for investment property. After all, statistically, investor loans on properties are more likely to default than home-owner loans because investors carry only a financial attachment to the property. (Homeowners usually have a financial and emotional attachment to their homes.) Because of the higher degree of default and higher perceived risk, investor loans generally are more difficult to obtain. Financial institutions that give investor loans generally have guidelines that put a lot of emphasis on the credit report. We suggest you meet with one or two lenders to determine if you qualify for investor loans and the types of loan products for which you qualify.

Financial institutions often offset their risk by requiring large down payments. Lenders don't get the lendees' *emotional* attachment to the property. Instead, they often try to get a large *cash* attachment. These institutions further offset their risk (like they do with most homeowner loans) by attaching the property to the loan—essentially using the property as collateral. That means if an investor gets in over his or her head and defaults on the loan, the financial institution receives the property to cover its losses.

Because homeowner loans are generally easier to obtain than investment loans, some investors have used them to buy their initial investment properties. However, these loans usually require the buyer to live in the property for a certain period of time (often two years). If you intend to use this option, factor this requirement into the equation.

Another way to access funds from a financial institution with your credit is with a line of credit. In this case, the lender usually gives you a preset amount of money that you can access whenever you need it. The most common type is a home equity loan, in which the loan is secured by the investor's home residence. The interest rates on these loans vary and may be lower than an investor loan. They usually aren't fixed but are tied to some index, such as the Federal Prime Rate.

Buyer **B**eware: **T**erms *of* **I**nvestor **L**oans

Be careful when using an investor loan to buy property. Not all loans are structured the same. In fact, a variety of terms and conditions can make them substantially different and your credit rating may or may not qualify you for certain ones. Assess the interest rate, fixed rate versus variable rate, the term to repay, the costs to obtain the loan, any prepayment penalties if you pay off the loan early, and all other aspects of the loans you are considering. All of these factors can substantially affect your profits.

When assessing the real estate investment strategy that meets your cash and credit resources, be sure to consider the differences in each. Again, for the Buy and Flip strategy, you may be able to grow your financial resources to buy more properties much faster than using the Buy and Hold strategy due to the periodic cash windfalls you receive when you flip houses. The Buy and Lease/Purchase strategy will likely fall somewhere in the middle regarding how much cash and credit you will require. Also, both the Buy and Hold and the Buy and Lease/Purchase strategies will require you to have cash or credit in reserve for property repairs and maintenance, as well as to pay expenses related to rerenting the properties, such as advertising and utilities.

If you choose a strategy of buying single-family houses, you will probably need a lot less cash and credit than if you buy multiplexes, apartment buildings, or office buildings. In your assessment, consider how low-income, middle-income, and high-income communities will impact your strategy. After all, purchasing properties in low-income communities would require less cash and credit than purchasing properties in high-income communities.

Finally, find ways to conserve your funds when you buy properties. For example, you could negotiate to have the seller pay closing costs and perhaps the repairs and improvements. Find out more about these and other cash-conserving tips in our free e-book, "Six and a Half Ways to Conserve Cash," at *www.Regular Riches.com/ConserveCash.*

THE RIGHT MINIMUM INVESTOR DISCOUNT FOR US

We would have loved to read a chapter like this before we began our real estate investing careers. Instead, we've had to learn many of these lessons from the school of hard knocks. We've tried all three investment strategies and a variety of Minimum Investor Discount Percentages, and we've determined the best strategy and MID% for our personal situation.

Before we walk you through our preferred investment strategy and MID%, we thought it would be helpful to share some of our experiences using the other two strategies to better help you decide which strategy will work best for you. Once we settled on our investment strategy, our Minimum Investor Discount Percentage was relatively easy for us to determine.

Buy and Flip Strategy

Initially, we chose the Buy and Flip strategy for our real estate investment business. We had known each other for only a few years and felt uncertain about entering into a long-term business relationship, so when we considered buying a property together, we planned to sell it as quickly as possible. However, after we purchased our first property at a big discount, our flip strategy didn't go according to plan.

Several months went by with no buyer—and our stress level went higher the longer the property went unsold. We tried just about everything. We played with the advertising by purchasing ads in different sectors, rewording them, using bold letters, and more. We tried different sign techniques by buying nicer signs and placing them at different points in the neighborhood. We even began to discount the price.

After several months and still no buyer, we felt like we were running out of options and our profits were at real risk. Continuing to pay the monthly mortgage payment, utility bills, and advertising costs, we believed that discounting the property any further would turn our first purchase into a loser.

Of more significance—and why this chapter is so important—if we had lost money on our first purchase, we likely wouldn't have purchased a second, third, and fourth property together. We would have lost our confidence, with only a money-loser to show for our first investment together. This story reflects the stories of many investors who give up on real estate for the wrong reasons. It's not that real estate is a bad investment vehicle. Rather, many investors either haven't taken the time to select the right investment strategy or haven't executed it properly. Again, this almost happened to us.

Fortunately, Scott suggested lease/purchasing the house. He had some background in this (as we'll discuss in our Buy and Hold experiences). We were reluctant at first, knowing this approach would require a longer-term business relationship than we'd planned. Here's the good news: The lease/purchase ad attracted a wonderful family within one week and they moved in within the month. During the time they lease/purchased the house from us, we received fair market rent and never had to repair or maintain the house (because the agreement required them to do so). They actually put in new carpet with their own money. Due to a job transfer, the family moved a year later. Again, we advertised and placed another family in the house within three weeks. The second family agreed to pay full Fair Market Value at the time we signed the lease/purchase, then bought the home about 18 months into their lease/purchase agreement. This gave us the confidence to buy more properties at a discount. We've been investing together as partners ever since.

Buy and Hold Strategy

Our firsthand experiences using a Buy and Hold strategy weren't as real estate partners. Andy obtained his experience with his primary residence by renting out his house and its lower-level apartment from time to time. Despite challenges, by and large, Andy has had a good experience with this strategy and earned decent profits to show for it. Still, Andy wouldn't favor the Buy and Hold strategy over the Buy and Lease/Purchase strategy due to the transient nature of most tenants and the resulting time, effort, stress, and headaches.

Scott's experience with the Buy and Hold strategy came in the 1980s when he began buying and renting low-income homes with his father, Denny. Scott had grown up around this business; his father had been buying these types of houses using the Buy and Hold strategy for many years. However, on February 13, 1986, less than a month after Scott had turned 20, his father was killed in a car accident. Scott and the rest of his family were devastated. His parents were divorced, he was the oldest child, and he became the executor of his father's estate. That not only meant that he'd have to decide what to do with the properties he had purchased with his father, but he had to determine what to do with his father's entire real estate portfolio (which was fairly large).

Scott's father did a lot of wonderful things for his family, including instilling confidence in all three of his children. This confidence—combined with years of real-life real estate management education—convinced Scott to keep his father's entire portfolio. From his father, he'd learned that real estate investing was a great vehicle for financial freedom. Scott believed that the investment he'd make when his father died would pay off for him and his family later on.

At the time, Scott shouldered the stress and obligations of college life while also managing multiple rental homes. Most tenants stayed for a year or two, though some stayed longer and others stayed only a short time. He dreaded checking the mailbox each month, then figuring out who he would have to hound for rent. Even worse, he hated getting phone calls at all hours of the day and night about maintenance problems. Further, it bothered him to give up part of his day to show a property to a prospective tenant, meet a repair person, or deal with other related headaches. Andy remembers Scott's bachelor party when one of his college roommates described how he remained fond of Scott despite the fact that the dorm phone would ring frequently—and at all hours of the night—from tenants calling. He laughed, saying he doubted any other undergraduates had to deal with similarly "popular" roommates.

During this period, Scott joined the Georgia Real Estate Investment Association, where he learned about the lease/purchase concept. Unfortunately, he wasn't able to apply this concept to most of his homes because his lower-income tenants simply weren't interested in buying or didn't appreciate the concept. Fortunately, he kept the houses rented with help from his brother, Brian, and sister, Marcy, and they eventually sold them at a nice profit. Even more significant, he learned that the Buy and Hold strategy wasn't for him.

Buy and Lease/Purchase Strategy

Based on the experience and knowledge we acquired over time, we've focused on the Buy and Lease/Purchase strategy. Acknowledging that it doesn't work well for certain types of properties, we only buy properties that work best for this strategy. (We'll review types of properties for Golden Key 2.) We also know that this strategy may not work well for people in partnerships due to its long-term nature.

If you're considering the Buy and Lease/Purchase strategy, we encourage you to save your own cash, build your own credit, and carefully choose your partner. The bottom line for us is that this strategy has significantly reduced the time, effort, stress, and headaches of our investing business. It has also led us to the six profit sources that the Buy and Flip and Buy and Hold strategies simply don't offer. This strategy is the right one for us and may be for you, too. You can learn more about this strategy in our book *Buy Low, Rent Smart, Sell High* and at our Web site (*www.RegularRiches.com*).

After selecting the Buy and Lease/Purchase strategy, our Minimum Investor Discount Percentage was relatively easy for us to choose. Because we want to make efficient use of our time and know that we have the other five profit sources working for us, *we use a MID% of 10 percent* in most cases.

By using the MID% at the lowest end of the range, we are able to cast a wider net to find properties. In other words, there are more properties that meet our Buy Even Lower criteria. Therefore, we don't have to spend as much money, time, and energy looking for our investments. This savings translates into more money, time, and energy to find more real estate investments and to enjoy our Regular Riches.

3

GOLDEN KEY 2—KNOW WHAT GOOD PROPERTIES LOOK LIKE

Before you even start to look at properties to Buy Even Lower, you need to determine what good properties look like. After all, you have literally millions of properties to choose from, so you should have a certain type of property in mind before you go looking. You can waste a lot of money, time, and energy if you don't, which obviously works against Buying Even Lower and achieving Regular Riches.

An important point: *A good property for one investor may be viewed as a bad property by another investor.* How can this be? Because different real estate investing strategies and Minimum Investor Discounts require different types of properties. For example, a residential investor will view a well-priced deal on a strip mall as a bad property for his or her investment strategy, while a commercial investor may view this same property as the deal of a lifetime. Additionally, one residential investor may view a duplex as a bad property for his or her single-family home strategy, while another views the duplex as a perfect fit for a multifamily unit strategy. Further, a Buy and Hold investor and a Buy and

Lease/Purchase investor may love what they see when they view a home with a 10 percent discount, while a Buy and Flip investor may view the home as unprofitable.

Accordingly, just like your investment strategy and personal situation helps determine your Minimum Investor Discount (Golden Key 1), they also play a big role in defining what a good property looks like for you. Additionally, while the other five golden keys in this book can be used to purchase just about any type of property at the appropriate discount, this golden key helps you sort through the multitude of property types. By doing so, you can focus on those that best fit your personal situation and deliver the profits you desire.

DEVELOPED VERSUS UNDEVELOPED PROPERTIES

You've probably heard stories about great riches mined by real estate developers. Some of the wealthiest real estate investors buy and develop land as a niche. Does the name Donald Trump ring a bell? Many people have bought undeveloped land and held it for years while it skyrocketed in value. Others have bought undeveloped land and quickly flipped it for quick profits. You might be thinking it would be fun to develop a property, then flip it, rent it, or lease/purchase it. All of the above scenarios are possible. However, we don't recommend inexperienced or part-time investors invest in undeveloped land off the bat.

Although there may be a substantial upside with undeveloped property, you generally face more risk with undeveloped rather than developed property. Investors of undeveloped property are able to visualize how an empty lot or piece of land filled with trees can eventually be a successful investment property with new buildings. Whether they plan to develop the land or not, these investors usually draw informed conclusions about the future development prospects of the property. They must see the physical transformation in their minds and on paper; they must have the ability to visualize the financial transformation to ensure there are profits at the end of the rainbow.

First, they have to assess the current value of the undeveloped land. This could be relatively easy if other undeveloped land around the property has been sold recently. However, assessing the value of undeveloped property may be more difficult if no comparative sales have occurred in the last few years or the piece of land is surrounded by developed property.

They then need to determine the value of the property once it is developed, plus the costs required to develop it. That task can be easier when the investor seeks to develop the property in conformance with the buildings around it. For example, if investors want to build one or more houses on property surrounded by similar houses, then they should be able to relatively easily understand the value of the fully developed property. On the other hand, if they choose to develop a structure different from those surrounding the property or if not much developed property exists in the vicinity, then arriving at this figure will be more difficult. Building houses next to office buildings or in an undeveloped rural community requires investors to make a more speculative decision on the final value of the property once it has been developed.

Determining the cost of developing the property may be the most complex task. Consider the initial costs associated with the property: architects, zoning issues, permits, clearing trees and other structures, grading the land, and attorney fees. Once the costs for getting the property ready for building are understood, they then need to fully assess all building costs, including sewers, roads, sidewalks, and building costs themselves. Finally, they must account for miscellaneous costs, such as payments on the loan while the property is under development, bringing utilities to the property, and marketing.

Once investors looking to develop the land (or flip it to a developer) understand the potential value of the developed property and estimates to develop it, they can determine potential profits. For savvy investors, big profits may await. Although this type of investing can be extremely profitable, all of these factors make these types of investments riskier and more challenging than buying developed properties. Investors who develop property usually must also make a significant "time and effort" investment and the cost can be extremely high. These make up the major reasons most investors don't buy undeveloped property with a plan to develop it.

If you're looking to Buy and Hold a piece of undeveloped property, costs and profits can vary significantly. On the one hand, if you buy in a rural area, the cost per acre may be relatively inexpensive. If you buy in an urban or suburban area, the cost will probably be higher. Different parts of the country also play a role in these costs. The biggest drawback of sitting on undeveloped land is paying the taxes while you receive little or no income until it's sold. Yes, there may be creative ways to generate some income, such as letting people cut down and buy trees off the land, grow food on the land, hunt on the land, and so on. However, the taxes that are due now and in the future may be significant and grow to be quite a burden. Therefore, these investors must make sure enough money will be available to cover them.

Finally, predicting the appreciation value of undeveloped land can be tricky. In rural areas, it can be many years before the value of the property increases while urban and suburban areas may see more rapid appreciation. In either instance, patience often produces profits—though it may take ten or more years, especially in rural areas.

Purchasing undeveloped land is best for those who are full-time investors and have the time and experience to do this properly. Part-time investors may also find the Buy and Hold strategy works for them with undeveloped property in rural communities, especially if they live close to the property, know the local trends, or plan to use the property for hunting, fishing, camping, and so on. Additionally, it's critical to understand zoning laws, taxes, and any other issues affecting the property (for example, whether it is on a floodplain, located close to a dump, etc.).

Yes, undeveloped properties can lead to significant profits for investors who have the vision and know what they're doing. However, we invest in developed property due to the significantly reduced complexity, risk, time, and effort associated with it. Many people have dreams of building something and have thought about what a piece of land would look like if it was transformed from a bunch of trees or an empty lot to a developed property with roads and buildings. However, it's one thing to dream about this. It's something substantially different to risk a big chunk of your time and money on it.

RESIDENTIAL VERSUS COMMERCIAL PROPERTIES

Our bet is that, because you're reading this book, you're leaning toward investing in residential real estate. After all, that's what the majority of people do. Yet, commercial real estate investing is also a viable way to generate wealth. Many people have made fortunes investing in commercial properties.

To compare and contrast residential versus commercial properties, let's start with the type most people are less familiar with: commercial properties. These properties (for example, strip centers and office buildings) are like residential properties—you can buy, rent, and sell them. In fact, many successful commercial property investors have large, positive monthly cash flows from the multiple rents, long tenant leases, and big profit payoffs when they sell these assets.

Though commercial properties can realize big rewards, the risks are usually bigger, too. Become well educated about these risks and how to deal with them before investing. You're usually dealing with a different set of players in the commercial arena. Buyers and sellers of commercial properties are usually full-time professionals who know how to get the most out of a deal. After all, their livelihood depends on it. Of course you may also see this with investors who own residential apartment building properties and banks who sell foreclosed residential properties (both of which we discuss in detail later in this book). But the majority of buyers and sellers of residential real estate are not full-time professionals. Therefore, most commercial investors need to really know their stuff or have a trusted advisor before buying. This was the primary reason Jill (Chapter 1) chose not to target commercial properties.

Another risk involves renting space and dealing with a different type of tenant than with residential properties. These tenants usually regard their rents as mere business transactions without having any emotional attachment to the property. For example, if they're short on money, they'll probably pay the bank holding a loan on their house first so they (and their kids) have a roof over their heads, and then pay the commercial landlord if they have any money left.

The commercial landlord–tenant laws are often different from residential landlord–tenant laws, providing more opportunities for missteps or confusion if you're doing both. The necessity for an involved (and costly) real estate attorney is also often far more significant in commercial transactions than in residential. For example, the repetitive nature of our residential investing has allowed us to generate the forms and legal agreements required to conduct our real estate business. We can use these agreements time and again with new tenants without involving our real estate attorney. Our attorney only gets involved when new issues arise that we haven't dealt with in the past, which is rare. Therefore, the complexity and variation of commercial transactions can increase the investor's legal costs.

Commercial property investing also forces most people to put more of their eggs in one basket, because the cost of most commercial property is usually greater than that of a residential house, condominium, or duplex. Of course, the cost depends on the size, location, and condition of the commercial property. And some residential properties, such as apartment buildings and quadplexes, can certainly cost a similar amount. However, by and large, the cost of most residential property transactions pales in comparison to most commercial property transactions. We strongly recommend that all investors diversify their portfolio by spreading their investments over multiple assets. So if you're short on cash and credit, lower-valued real estate purchases are the best way to diversify—and residential properties usually provide a greater opportunity for this than do commercial.

Commercial property investors almost always require renting their units to tenants rather than using the lease/purchase model we favor. That means these investors are rarely able to get the same tenant commitment that a rent-to-buy tenant will give a property as a result of their emotional and financial attachment. Although some commercial property units are large enough for the landlord to shift maintenance and repair responsibilities to the tenant, landlords with smaller units usually must maintain these responsibilities along with the costs and headaches. This often necessitates a part-time or full-time property manager.

In Good Times and Bad, People Need a Place to Live
Consider, too, that in both good and bad times, people always need a place to live. On the other hand, businesses can grow quickly in good times, yet can shrink even faster in bad times, causing them to default on their leases. While companies sometimes lay off many employees at the snap of a finger, you simply can't downsize your family. For example, if your tenants are a family with two kids and they're living in a rental home that meets their needs in a neighborhood where their kids love growing up, the last thing they want to do is move to a smaller home in an unfamiliar neighborhood. *People tend to downsize their home residences as an absolute last resort.* Consequently, residential real estate tends to be more stable than commercial real estate.

Although commercial properties can generate great wealth for investors who know what they're doing, we choose to invest solely in residential real estate. As relatively conservative investors, the risks we describe for commercial properties have kept us away from investing in them so far. We especially like that residential property works best for our Buy and Lease/Purchase strategy, allows us to easily diversify our portfolio, and is more stable than commercial property. If we ever choose to invest in a commercial property, rest assured we'd do our homework and learn more about this investment than most people learn before they buy their first residential property.

SINGLE-FAMILY VERSUS MULTIFAMILY PROPERTIES

Deciding to invest in residential instead of commercial property is an easy decision for many investors. However, choosing between single-family and multifamily properties is one of the toughest decisions many real estate investors make.

Scott actually owned several duplexes early in his real estate investing career. Multifamily properties, such as duplexes, triplexes, and quadplexes as well as condominiums, town homes, and apartment buildings can be good real estate investment vehicles. Why? They tend to cost less to purchase per square foot than single-family properties in the same community and they offer other cost efficiencies from the landlord's perspective. For example, two simultaneous vacancies in an apartment complex can be advertised in one ad. The investor can also show both units on the same day without making separate trips, which he or she can't do for two single-family homes in different parts of town.

Also, multifamily properties usually cost less to build because they're literally built next to or on top of each other. They don't come with a yard surrounding each home and have lower construction costs than single-family because they often share walls, ceilings, or floors. They also may cost less to repair and maintain because maintenance people or companies may discount their work in return for volume on the close-together properties. Some investors simply hire a full-time repair person.

In summary, the costs of multifamily properties are usually spread across the properties located next to or on top of each other. Additionally, though the multifamily properties frequently rent for less than a single-family property with comparable square footage, when managed properly, the property's profits can be vast.

Unless you live in a big city like New York, San Francisco, or Chicago, most communities don't have a large number of multi-family properties because, if given the choice, most people prefer to live in single-family houses. As a result, the small pool of prop-erties to buy may lead to more competition for each property, which may drive up the price.

Although multifamily properties may cost less per square foot to build, investors who purchase multifamily properties often need to pay substantially more for each purchase because, unlike a single-family home purchase, the investor is buying multiple family homes at one time. This higher price for multifamily prop-erties can lead to longer listing periods when selling investment properties. Also, sellers may be limited in marketing their multi-family property to another investor. Buyers looking to live in the property often don't have the interest or the funds to purchase a multifamily property. Because investors of these types of proper-ties tend to be landlords of multiple homes and properties, they also may need to work full-time to manage the properties or hire a manager.

Multifamily properties are hard to flip due to the small pool of potential buyers and are rarely lease/purchased. However, they are often the right choice for investors who want to be in the rental business. One scary thought: We have heard of situations in which angry tenants have banded together to team up against landlords, which you rarely see with single-family homes (unless the tenants are located in the same neighborhood).

Although multifamily properties can offer good profit oppor-tunities, we prefer single-family properties—specifically single-fam-ily houses (rather than condominiums or town houses). We like that there is a big supply of these properties available to purchase and they are easier to sell in our community. We also like that we can spread our investments among more properties to diversify our portfolio. Additionally, the residential, single-home properties work well with our Buy and Lease/Purchase strategy.

HOUSES, APARTMENTS, AND CONDOMINIUM PROPERTIES

Whether you invest in houses, apartments, condominiums, or town homes, a savvy investor can find ways to profit from each. However, each has its particular characteristics, which you should be aware of before investing in any of them.

Apartments tend to be right for investors who are in the rental business and are looking to buy a multifamily property. As we discussed in the previous section, investors generally must invest significantly more money at one time than an investor buying an individual house or condominium. Additionally, unlike most sellers and buyers of individual houses and condominiums, the apartment building sellers and buyers are often sophisticated, full-time investors or an investment company. Also, the length of time to sell an apartment building is generally much longer than for a house or condominium because the larger sales price results in a smaller pool of buyers.

Condominiums and town homes tend to be right for investors living in communities with a limited supply of single-family homes or investors looking to invest less money per square foot than they would for a house with similar square footage. Condominiums and town homes tend to sell for less than houses because they lack space between the residences.

For the investor interested in using the rental or lease/purchase model, condominiums come with the convenience of no upkeep for the roof, yard, and community areas. However, they usually have the added cost of an association fee to cover such expenses. Note that these monthly fees can add up to more money than if the investor directly hired workers to complete the maintenance and repair.

Like single-family houses, condominiums can usually be easily rented, lease/purchased, or flipped in a good market. This is what Jill did in Chapter 1. However, for the same reasons condominiums tend to cost less to buy than houses, they also tend to rent and sell for less, too. Additionally, in a bad market, we have seen how the value of condominiums drops significantly faster than houses in most communities. One reason is that when real estate prices fall, many of the stable condominium owners shift to houses, which have suddenly become more affordable and are often their first choice.

Although apartments and condominiums can be great for certain savvy investors, we prefer to keep our risk low and our life simple. Houses allow us to invest our money in what we believe is the most stable, least risky type of real estate.

We believe houses are the most stable because they are part of the American Dream. Most people simply dream of owning one. Therefore, whether you're renting, lease/purchasing, or flipping, you are usually casting your widest net when you leverage these types of properties. Unlike buying an apartment building, we don't have to worry about getting overextended or too dependent on one property. Further, unlike buying a condominium, we don't have to worry as much about a bad real estate market or mismanaged condo funds and surprise condo fee assessments. In sum, we have found that single-family houses allow us to minimize our risk and worries.

PROPERTIES IN LOW-INCOME, MIDDLE-INCOME, AND HIGH-INCOME NEIGHBORHOODS

In our lengthy real estate investing careers, we have invested in low-income, middle-income, and high-income neighborhoods. In fact, as mentioned earlier, Scott's entire portfolio consisted of low-income homes when he first started out investing. Through the years, we have purchased (both individually and together) our fair share of houses in middle-income and high-income neighborhoods.

Whether a property is located in a low-income, middle-income, or high-income neighborhood has nothing to do with the amount of profit a particular property generates. Rather, it has everything to do with the income of the typical person who would be interested in renting or buying that property. The typical renter or buyer's income is important because it sets the tone for the type of property, relative to the others in the community. It's important to understand that the absolute purchase price of a property is not as important as its purchase price relative to others in the community. Because most communities have low-income, middle-income, and high-income residents, you need to understand what type of renter or buyer the particular property is likely to attract. This is why selecting your real estate investment strategy at the beginning of the Buy Low process makes a huge difference in determining what "a good property" looks like.

If you're going to be a Buy and Flip investor, you probably will want to focus on buying middle-income and high-income properties because low-income properties usually carry a much lower discount in terms of total dollars simply due to their lower value relative to the other types of properties. Therefore, though some investors do make good money in low-income property flipping, they usually have to work harder to find deep discounts and they have to complete more deals to get the same total profits that middle-income and high-income property flippers are able to achieve. Additionally, a large percentage of low-income people are simply interested in renting (it's all they have ever known), so the pool of buyers is usually smaller than for middle-income and high-income properties. In fact, many investors in low-income houses often sell their properties to other investors.

If you're going to rent properties as a Buy and Hold investor, then you probably want to focus on buying properties in low-income and middle-income neighborhoods. Properties aimed at high-income renters usually require such a high rent to be profitable that few potential renters can afford them. Most high-income people are looking to buy a property, not rent it. The high-income renters tend to be short-term corporate relocations and people who are cash strapped or credit challenged.

Because we lease/purchase our properties—a hybrid of the flipping and pure renting formulas—we prefer middle-income properties. We've tried our lease/purchase program with the other two types of properties but have found the above challenges hold true.

In fact, most of the properties Scott's father left him when he passed away were low-income properties. After a while, Scott decided to try and lease/purchase them as a way to sell off some of his portfolio. However, most of his renters were simply not interested in the opportunity to own these homes through a lease/purchase program, preferring to simply rent. Even though some signed up for the lease/purchase program, few exercised this option. In the end, Scott sold most of the low-income properties to other investors. Therefore, we believe that low-income properties are best as pure rentals.

On the other hand, when we've tried to lease/purchase high-income properties they have simply attracted too little interest. Our experience has been that most people in this income bracket can usually afford to buy a property. Further, their peer group expects them to do so. Additionally, the short-term corporate relocation people are usually interested in simply renting. This leaves the small pool of cash-strapped and credit-challenged high-income people. Though the profits are potentially greater with high-income people, we have had a great deal of problems when we've attempted to lease/purchase high-income properties.

In sum, we prefer middle-income properties. We've found that the majority of the people in this income group strive to own their own home. Plus, there is a large pool of people in this income bracket who are willing to commit to a rent-to-buy program. Often, they are interested because they are cash strapped or credit challenged; sometimes it is simply because they are making the transition from being a low-income to middle-income household; and other times they're just starting out (for example, newlyweds, first job out of college, etc.). The bottom line is that middle-income properties work extremely well for our Buy and Lease/Purchase investment strategy.

URBAN, SUBURBAN, AND RURAL PROPERTIES

Depending on where you live, there are a variety of considerations specific to your geography that you may need to consider. Do you live in a big urban city, a suburb, or a rural town? How far from where you live are the different types of properties in which you're considering to invest?

Big urban centers like New York City, Chicago, Los Angeles, and San Francisco often offer many multifamily options, such as condominiums and apartments, and loads of office buildings. Suburbs usually have large numbers of single-family houses and may also have a good supply of multifamily properties, office buildings, and strip centers. Rural communities tend to have a fair number of single-family houses and may have a smattering of multifamily properties, strip centers, and office buildings. Therefore, if you choose to focus on properties in your community, your options as to the types of properties to choose from may be limited.

Though there are hundreds, if not thousands, of properties that meet our investing criteria, we choose to pass up on most that are not within 30 minutes of where we live (based on weekend driving time, not rush hour). The farthest-away property we ever purchased was 60 minutes from our home residences. We generally look for a bigger discount when the property is farther away. For most of our investing partnership, Andy has lived in Atlanta (a large urban city) and Scott has lived in Dunwoody (a

Tips for Investing Outside Your Community

If your community doesn't offer enough of the properties in which you would like to focus your real estate investing, then you may choose to venture outside of your community. You may choose to look at a map to assess the geography, or simply get in the car or take a train and venture into an unfamiliar town. Perhaps you have heard about another community with the types of properties you're looking for. We have done this, and it can be valuable to help you better appreciate the properties in your community and learn about ones outside of your community.

A word of caution if you venture outside of your community: The farther away you venture, the greater the risk you take on. First, your unfamiliarity with another community may cause you to invest in an area in which properties are positioned to decrease in value without you fully understanding the negative dynamics. Second, the farther away, the harder it is to keep an eye on your investment. Your investment properties are always at more risk when you don't keep tabs on them.

medium-size suburb of Atlanta). Accordingly, we invest in single-family houses and we choose to buy properties in the suburbs (such as Dunwoody, Marietta, Roswell, and Alpharetta). The good news for both of us is that we've been able to find plenty of single-family houses within a 30-minute drive of our homes.

BEDROOMS, BATHROOMS, AND OTHER FEATURES IN PROPERTIES

Properties come with different features. Residential properties can have one, two, three, or more bedrooms and bathrooms. Some properties have a big backyard, large kitchen, bonus room, basement, pool, or another extra feature. Some are ranch houses while others are two stories. Some have brick exteriors, while others are stucco or wood. The list of features a property can have is seemingly endless and can be confusing to investors.

Which features might be more significant to potential buyers and renters in your community? How much value should be attached to missing or extra features? Is this particular feature really worth the extra $10,000 the seller wants for the property? Preselecting your real estate investment strategy as well as the general community in which you choose to invest can simplify your analysis immensely.

For example, if you're a Buy and Flip investor who focuses on buying and selling houses in high-income neighborhoods, then you may want to buy houses with a minimum of four bedrooms, three bathrooms, a basement, pool, and big yard. However, if you're a Buy and Hold investor focusing on buying and renting condominiums in a busy urban community, you may choose to focus on units with one or two bedrooms and one or two bathrooms. On the other hand, if you're a Buy and Lease/Purchase investor choosing to cater to families in the suburbs, you'll probably want to buy homes with at least three bedrooms, two bathrooms, and a decent yard. Therefore, choosing your investment strategy and community to buy in at the beginning of the Buy Low process will help you focus on certain features.

Also, get to know the community in which you intend to invest because the easiest properties for most investors to work with are those with features that people in the community are used to buying and renting. If a property is missing one or more of these "must-have" features, you may substantially shrink your pool of buying and renting candidates. On the other hand, if you have extra features, you're at risk of not being compensated adequately for them.

For example, you may be a flipper focusing on affluent neighborhoods where most of the homes in the community have swimming pools and tennis courts. In this case, you probably want to buy homes with pools and tennis courts. Otherwise your available potential buyers may shrink substantially. On the other hand, if you're renting in an urban community with nice but not-too-upscale condominiums, you may not want to buy units with tremendously upscale finishes and bedrooms. Even though these units could rent for more, your incremental profits will probably not be high enough. If you're lease/purchasing homes in a suburban community that typically don't have basements, you probably don't want to buy homes with basements. Again, you probably won't be properly compensated for this feature.

With all that being said, some investors believe that properties lacking in a particular feature may actually be more profitable. In some cases, we believe this is correct. For example, we've found that there are often greater discounts on properties lacking in one or more feature. Our Buy and Lease/Purchase investing strategy allows us to rent and sell properties based on "fair" lease/purchase terms (rent is applied toward the purchase price, residents have up to three years to close with a locked-in purchase price at the time the lease/purchase agreement is signed, etc.), and less on the specific features of the home. Therefore, if your real estate investing strategy is conducive to buying properties that lack certain features and you know how to properly evaluate and value them, then you may not need to avoid buying these properties and actually may look for them.

Again, our real estate investing strategy is built around lease/purchasing single-family houses in suburban communities. Most of the communities we invest in predominantly consist of houses with three bedrooms, two bathrooms, and minimum one-car garage. Therefore, almost all the houses we buy have these minimum features (or the houses can be improved without much difficulty to add these minimum features). When it comes to the other features, we like flat lots, brick homes, good-size yards, and basements. We've found that our lease/purchase formula usually attracts tenant/buyers focused more on the terms of our rent-to-buy program than on the particular features of the home. Additionally, we know how to value these houses. Therefore, houses that may be missing a feature often make our best buying opportunities.

In Chapter 1, Jill found that two-bedroom, two-bathroom condominiums were hot for buying and flipping in her community. Therefore, she targeted these types of properties.

HOME RESIDENCE VERSUS VACATION PROPERTIES

Vacation properties, such as properties on the beach, the lake, in the mountains, in a resort, even in another country, can be profitable and especially fun for the investor to use. These types of properties often do extremely well in good economic times. However, the values of many of these properties may drop like a lead balloon in bad economic times. Therefore, compared to most home residence properties (single-family homes, multi-plex units, apartments, etc.), vacation properties are considered by many to be fairly risky investments, especially in the short term.

Therefore, vacation properties are often best for those investors who will use the properties throughout the year and will hold onto them for a relatively long period of time. The use aspect of this investment by the investor, unlike almost every other type of investment discussed in this chapter, produces additional types of value that can be used in your return-on-investment formula. First, by staying in your own beach or ski resort house when on vacation, you will save significant dollars versus what you would pay to rent the same property. Second, because you own it, you can remodel and decorate this place exactly the way you want to meet your family's needs. In short, vacation properties offer an added value that other home-residence properties don't offer.

Looking strictly at the investment aspect, because vacation properties are rarely local, investors who purchase them often have to hire management companies to rent the property when the investors aren't using them or to simply keep an eye on them while they're away. If an investor chooses not to use a management company, then he or she may have to drive hours or even fly to the property to rent it, check up on the property, or tend to any maintenance problems. These costs can be both financial and psychological.

Although vacation properties may be great for the Buy and Hold investor looking for property to rent, they are usually not

The **E**motional **C**osts of **V**acation **P**roperties

Unlike other investments, renting your vacation home can carry with it some emotional costs because the renters inevitably won't treat your vacation home like theirs. Accordingly, you will have to fix and replace items that would have lasted longer if only your family had used them. You may not want to leave sentimental objects, such as Aunt Bonnie's 100-year-old antique vase or Uncle Brad's World Series autographed baseball on the coffee table when you're not there.

Another consideration with vacation properties is that they often tug at the investor for use or visitation. In other words, while the investor might want to vacation in other places, visit friends or family, or simply stay in the primary residence and relax for the weekend, a nagging thought to use the vacation property is often in the back of the investor's mind. Accordingly, many investors forgo some of these places they might otherwise visit, in order to make regular visits to their vacation property.

for the Buy and Flip, Buy and Lease/Purchase, or even standard rental investors. Though some Buy and Flip investors can make significant profits from vacation properties, most investors who try this find it difficult because the best time to profit from these is in good economic times. During these times, there is usually significant competition. Therefore, the big discounts (25 percent or more) necessary to make the flipper investor's business model work are often hard to come by. On the other hand, during bad economic times the flipper investor will probably find a lot of discount vacation properties. However, profits from selling them also will be hard to come by because many people consider vacation properties a luxury item and people tend to buy fewer luxury items during bad economic periods.

As for Buy and Lease/Purchase investors, though these properties can theoretically be lease/purchased like any other property, most tenants for these properties are short timers, renting for one to two weeks or up to several months at a time. Therefore, the lease/purchase model usually does not work for this type of property.

Also, keep in mind that standard rental properties have tenants who lease for at least a year. With vacation properties, people look to rent for relatively short periods of time: a week or two, or several months at most. Therefore, many different tenants coming and going will probably lead to extra repair and maintenance costs as well as replacing furnishings. There is also the extra time and cost (especially if you hire a management company) to market and sign contracts with multiple tenants throughout the year. Finally, many vacation properties are seasonal—there are certain times of year when they are in higher demand. Vacation properties in ski resorts rent better during the winter, while properties along the coast in Florida are busiest during the late fall and winter months. These properties also tend to be in higher demand during holidays. Accordingly, the vacation property investor must be able to adjust and deal with the seasonal ups and downs, both with the amount of rent charged and the likely vacancy periods.

If you're interested in investing in vacation properties and don't want to use a management company, we recommend reading *Profit from Your Vacation Home Dream* by Christine Karpinski. You'll find a lot of valuable guidance for the do-it-yourself vacation property investor.

Although investors can reap good profits and provide many years of their family's enjoyment with vacation properties, we prefer to invest in home-residence properties within 30 minutes of our homes because they fit much better into our Buy and Lease/Purchase investment strategy. They tend to have long-term tenants, we don't furnish the properties, we don't have big price and vacancy fluctuations, and we can easily rent and keep an eye on our properties. Additionally, we like the relatively simple, straightforward real estate profits associated with this strategy.

MINT-CONDITION VERSUS UGLY AND AWFUL PROPERTIES

Many people like to buy properties that are in mint condition and ready for moving in, considering these "perfect" properties. These properties usually take a lot less time, energy, and headaches to flip, rent, and lease/purchase. For these reasons, mint-condition properties are usually in much higher demand and bring on increased competition from other investors, as well as those looking to live in or use them for their business. As a result, mint-condition properties often have significantly less discounting opportunities.

On the other hand, "ugly and awful" properties, which require significant repairs or have glaring faults (bad floor plans, built on a steep hill, situated in a ditch, etc.), often attract few buyers and are usually not in high demand. Most people simply don't know how to or don't want to deal with their imperfections. Others simply can't see their hidden beauty. Accordingly, ugly and awful properties often are significantly discounted and often provide investors great opportunities to obtain their Minimum Investor Discount.

When buying ugly and awful properties, make sure you factor all of the property's deficiencies into your offer with an extra premium for your willingness to accept and deal with all of its imperfections. Also, take the time to adequately understand the property's repair problems or faults. You may need to get estimates from contractors to determine the costs to fix them. Additionally, you may want to talk to people in the community (for example, real estate agents) to determine the significance of the imperfections relative to similar properties.

Yes, mint-condition properties are generally easier to deal with, both in the purchase phase and resell, rent, or lease/purchase phase. However, they often do not provide the kind of profit opportunities investors need. On the other hand, when managed properly, ugly and awful properties can be dealt with relatively easily and can be the source of immense profits.

During our many years of real estate investing, we have become good at recognizing the potential in handling ugly and awful properties. We take the time to adequately understand their repairs and faults. We then make sure that the property is properly discounted and that we are properly compensated for dealing with it. As a result, looking back at our investing career, ugly and awful properties have been absolutely "beautiful" on our bottom line.

We then use our Buy and Lease/Purchase strategy, set forth in our book, *Buy Low, Rent Smart, Sell High,* to obtain our profits. Of particular importance as described for Golden Key 1, we structure our lease/purchase program to be a win-win for us and the lease/purchaser. Accordingly, the terms we use play a significant role in our ability to get these ugly and awful properties rented/sold very quickly and efficiently. Yes, in many cases, it has been our ability to see the hidden beauty of a property and make the necessary repairs and improvements that contribute to our success. However, we believe that in many other cases, the lease/purchasers have chosen to overlook certain imperfections with the property due to the attractiveness of our lease/purchase terms.

Because ugly and awful properties have had such a significant impact on our ability to consistently find properties to Buy Even Lower and grow our profits, we've compiled some real-life stories about ugly and awful properties we've purchased and profited from. For all of these properties we received a significantly greater discount than our Minimum Investor Discount of 10 percent. These stories illustrate that there are a multitude of different types of ugly and awful properties, and many ways to deal with them. Hopefully, these stories will help provide you the insights and confidence you need when you have opportunities to buy them. Later in the book, for Golden Key 4—Calculate Maximum Purchase Prices, we show you how to mathematically assess these properties to determine the additional discount you should receive for dealing with them.

Real-Life Example 1: The Quick Fixer-Upper

One year, we previewed a postforeclosure property in December. The property was a typical starter house that required significant repairs: new flooring, paint, kitchen appliances, a heating and air-conditioning unit, ceiling fans, and other odds and ends. Because the home needed a cosmetic makeover, most families viewing it either couldn't see its hidden beauty or didn't want to mess with it. Also, the kitchen is an important feature for many people, so a lot of potential buyers were probably turned off by the out-of-date kitchen. This ugly and awful home to most who viewed it was sheer beauty to us. We knew that new flooring and paint throughout, updated kitchen appliances, and a proper cooling system would do the trick.

After we made our initial offer, it took one week and two counteroffers before we reached an agreement that included an appropriate discount with the seller. The purchase date was set for Wednesday, January 10. We estimated five to seven days of work before the house would be in condition to show. We don't believe in wasting time, so our contractors began work the afternoon of the closing. A sign went up out front immediately, and we began running our newspaper ad on Saturday, January 13. Our goal? To show the house the next weekend.

We were finished with the work as scheduled and did, in fact, show the property the weekend of January 21. We received two applications and selected a nice family who didn't need to move in until March 1, but agreed to meet us partway. We signed the lease on January 24 and it took effect February 14. We were making solid profits just 35 days after purchasing this ugly and awful property turned beautiful.

Real-Life Example 2: The Problem Property

No story better illustrates our philosophy that we sell terms first and the actual physical property a distant second. The right lease/purchaser recognizes this. In this case, we purchased a postforeclosure that didn't need repairs or improvements. Even the carpet was in acceptable condition. The ugly and awful news was that the house was the smallest in the neighborhood, didn't have a finished basement like the other homes, and had a small backyard bordered by a retention pond. These ugly and awful characteristics provided the perfect Buy Even Lower opportunity and made it the type of home we love for the right price. Fortunately, this property had been on the market for almost a year and we received a large discount on it.

Because the house didn't require any repairs, we placed the ad before our closing date to generate advance response. We received sufficient response the first weekend and the seller allowed us to show the property before our scheduled closing date.

Andy showed the house to four families and, as the last family was leaving, the Maas family pulled up in their minivan. Andy recalls his surprise as he noticed Mr. Maas couldn't have been more than 25 years old but he already had four children: a stepdaughter and three natural children. Later we learned that having so many children was the basis for the Maas's credit problems and the reason they were a great lease/purchase candidate. The Maases had married young and their needs got ahead of their income capabilities. Mr. Maas had solid employment and both were in the process of cleaning up the credit mistakes sometimes associated with youth.

The next two minutes proved to be some of the most amazing of our real estate career. The Maas family walked up to the front door and Andy came out to greet them. Mrs. Maas and the children went around, under, and over Andy as they moved through the front doorway with excitement and eagerness. Andy laughed as he heard the kids behind yelling and already staking their claims to the bedrooms.

Mr. Maas stood in the doorway and smiled at his family's exuberance. Andy greeted him warmly and handed him one of our flyers, which displays features of the house but more important, the key terms and conditions of our lease/purchase agreement.

Mr. Maas studied the flyer, looked up at Andy, then down at the flyer again. Finally, he looked up at Andy and said, "We'll take it!"

Andy was at a complete loss for how to handle this situation. After some stuttering, he mustered, "Don't you want to look at the house first?" Mr. Maas said he knew the neighborhood and, more important, our terms were good for him and his family and unlike anything he had seen during his house search. He joked that, from the comments he heard from his wife and kids, he had no doubt they liked the house. Andy calmly and politely explained to him that we have a process and we must select him (not the other way around). We would be happy to consider selecting his family but he had to first fill out a lease/purchase application. Mr. Maas then took a quick walk through the house, spoke with his wife, and filled out the application.

The Maas family proved to be a perfect fit for our program. Interestingly, we almost lost this opportunity due to a technicality. Normally, we take two to four business days to assess and select the right lease/purchaser, then set the move-in date within 15 to 30 days after the contract is signed. The Maases wanted to sign the contract immediately, which brought up a comical and unanticipated problem. Legally, we couldn't sign a contract to a house that we didn't yet own (the closing date was still two days away). We explained the situation to them, and they were willing to risk the delay and waited to sign the contract until after we closed on our purchase.

We later learned the explanation for the Maas's eagerness to lease/purchase a house Mr. Maas didn't even preview. The Maas family had found another lease/purchase opportunity. They simply wanted to lock up our lease/purchase before they had to commit to another. They told us that, with the other program, they had to come up with a $6,000 down payment and $6,000 more after six months, then they only had one year to purchase that house. If he didn't purchase within the first year, he'd forfeit the entire $12,000 and the landlord had no obligation to extend the purchase option. We've heard of many similar lease/purchase opportunities provided by other investors.

It's unlikely they could have found the money to make a purchase under the other agreement and would have lost $12,000 in the process. With us, the Maas family only had to come up with the first month's rent, a security deposit, and option money, which totaled less than $5,000. They had up to three years to exercise our lease/purchase and the sales price was locked in on the day they signed the lease. They actually exercised the purchase option during the middle of the second year of our lease/purchase agreement. Again, it's the strength and fairness of the lease/purchase terms that often turns an ugly and awful home into a beauty.

Real-Life Example 3: The House on the Hill

This house had been foreclosed on by a bank and unsuccessfully marketed for four months. It sat atop a hill with what must have been a 45-degree slope. It was a lot of work to walk up it. The backyard was flat but went back only five feet to a retaining wall. In short, it had no functional yard in back and required a workout to get to the front door. No wonder this house wasn't selling.

Rather than avoiding it like most homebuyers, we went after it aggressively and at our pricing. We stressed the negative curb appeal of the property when we sought—and received—a huge discount. While this wasn't the easiest house to market, our attractive lease/purchase terms offset the physical deficiencies of the property.

As anticipated, the marketing task for this house paralleled the slope of the front yard: an upward climb. It was almost comical. Each weekend, we averaged several solid appointments. As usual, one of us arrived at the house 30 minutes before the lease/purchasers were due to arrive. We turned on all the lights, ceiling fans, and the air-conditioning. Then we sat and waited. In this house, we experienced something unique.

Inside, we watched as many of our prepped and eager lease/purchase candidates drove up to the house, stopped their cars, waited for 30 to 60 seconds, then drove off. As special as our terms were, so many people were so incredibly turned off by the degree of the slope that, even after driving to the house, they had no interest in coming in and viewing the property.

However, we had anticipated this and that played into both our purchase price and also the special lease/purchase terms we offered. Eventually, we found a nice family. This ugly and awful purchase is, to this day, one of our most profitable.

Real-Life Example 4: The House in the Ditch

A close second to the house on the hill, the house in the ditch, presented a real marketing challenge to us. The house at 46 Denny Street sat at the bottom of a downward-sloping driveway— not a long, curvy driveway that gradually sloped downward over a large and well-landscaped front yard. You couldn't even see the house from the street.

Andy remembers one of the first prospective tenants who came by to view the house had a large car that he affectionately referred to as a *boat*. As he turned from the street onto the drive-way, the slope was so steep the bottom of his car scraped the road. He quickly reversed his car and parked on the street since his car couldn't make it down the driveway (Actually, the car may have made it down but might not have made it back up.)

The rest of the driveways on this street all sloped downward, but none to the degree of our house. All the other houses were visible from the street but the only evidence 46 Denny Street existed was the number on the mailbox.

Of course, we thought the unusual slope of the driveway and positioning of the house beyond view from the street might pose a difficulty during the marketing phase. Surprisingly, we had none. We purchased the home at a substantial discount and two weeks after we started running our ad we found a good family to lease/purchase the property. About 18 months later, the husband's employer transferred the family to another state and we easily found a new family to lease/purchase the property. The second family eventually exercised their purchase option and bought the property. This turned into one of our most successful lease/purchase investments because we realized all six of the Buy Low, Rent Smart, Sell High profit sources in our program.

Real-Life Example 5: The House on the Busy Street

We used to wonder why anyone would purchase a house directly on a busy street or main thoroughfare. Most people seem to prefer the peace and quiet that comes with a house that sits off the main street. Also, families with children rarely want to live on a high-traffic street. For these reasons, when we first saw 7890 Warner Way, we were not immediately excited about the property.

However, we were able to secure a healthy discount on the purchase. Therefore, we could offer a significantly reduced lease payment. This factor kept response to our ad at a healthy level, attracting plenty of people during the marketing phase. Still, not one family with kids who were less than ten years of age filled out an application.

The Russo family had only one child remaining at home, who was already out of high school, so they had little concern about safety issues related to the house's proximity to the street. Plus, its other attributes appealed to the Russos. More important, the Russos loved our lease/purchase terms. Warner Way was just the house they were looking for.

This problem property was a good deal for us because most traditional buyers were scared away by the close proximity to the main thoroughfare. Our lease/purchase program simply gave us that edge to turn this losing property into a winner.

Real-Life Example 6: The Ugliest House in the Subdivision—by Far!

The house at 687 Lori Lane was easily the ugliest one in the Carrie subdivision filled with cookie-cutter, small, simple three-bedroom and four-bedroom, two-and-a-half-bathroom starter houses. Almost all the homes in this subdivision had a brick exterior. However, this house had an odd rock and wood exterior. Furthermore, this house was only one house removed from the main street. Last, most of the other houses in Carrie were two-story traditional houses, while 687 Lori Lane was a one-story, ranch-style house. It had a large finished basement that made it comparable in living space to the other homes in the subdivision. However, from the street, it looked noticeably different and smaller than the other houses in the neighborhood.

For these reasons, Lori Lane wasn't selling. As usual, we weren't shy about pointing out the deficiencies in the property when negotiating our purchase price. We purchased the property significantly below market and in no time had found a family who loved our lease/purchase terms.

We've purchased a lot of houses similar to this one—houses that were among the least attractive in their neighborhoods. One of the most exciting attributes of these ugly and awful properties is that they often ride the coattails of the other properties in the neighborhood. In other words, they appreciate along with all the other properties in the neighborhood. Therefore, the positives from the good lease/purchase terms and the good neighborhood can turn the ugliest house in the neighborhood into a real beauty.

Real-Life Example 7: The House by the Railroad Tracks

Picture a nice family spending the first night in their new dream house. The oldest son, Dennis, has stayed up late playing on the computer. His younger sister, Danielle, is dreaming of tennis, while his younger brother, David, is dreaming of baseball.

Their baby sister, Diana, is dreaming of riding her bike. Their parents, Scott and Marie, are sound asleep in the master bedroom. All of a sudden the ground shakes and a loud noise awakens the entire household. A train passes through on tracks no more than 200 feet from the house. All of the children run into their parents' room crying and the entire family can't get back to sleep for another hour.

Families with children often make great lease/purchaser tenants because it's more difficult to uproot an entire family than single adults. In other words, the kids get settled into schools, make neighborhood friends, and provide an incentive for the parents to do everything they can to stay in the house and keep from defaulting on the lease/purchase agreement. Knowing this, we purchased this house on 8421 Evelyn Way, even though we knew the railroad tracks could be a significant deterrent to families.

Fortunately, a single man answered our ad. Joe McGuinness was holding down a high-profile consulting job. He wasn't able to purchase the property outright at the time because a small apartment unit he'd recently purchased as an investment was tying up his available credit. He and his friends would live in the house but the lease/purchase would be exclusively in his name.

Mr. McGuinness was a sharp, upwardly mobile guy. A man with a plan. This house by the railroad tracks was perfect for him and his friends. He didn't fit our typical lease/purchaser profile. However, his qualifications checked out and we were impressed with him.

As we anticipated, Mr. McGuinness followed through on 8421 Evelyn Way. In the second year of the lease/purchase agreement, he bought this house. The railroad tracks unquestionably scared away most potential homeowners, as well as most of our investor competition. But for us, it was just another profitable house purchase.

Real-Life Example 8: The Unfinished House

We purchased the house at 90 Brian Street in the Whitney subdivision from a bank that had foreclosed on a homebuilder's loan. The subdivision was almost complete, with the last four houses still under construction. The oldest house in the subdivision was no more than five years old. One of the homebuilders had gone bankrupt and left this house on Brian Street unfinished. The entire outside was complete, as was the frame and drywall inside, plus the plumbing and the electrical wiring. The only items that needed to be finished were installing the fixtures and appliances in the kitchen and bathrooms, installing flooring throughout the house, and painting the interior.

The bank was predictably having difficulty getting rid of this house but we saw this as a wonderful purchase opportunity. After all, why would a regular homebuyer purchase such a place in a neighborhood where new houses were still available? More specifically, since nothing inside was complete, the house was devoid of any interior physical qualities for a prospective homebuyer to fall in love with. We did the calculations and locked in a significant Total Investor Discount. We finished the project, then quickly lease/purchased this house.

No homeowners had wanted this project and the other investors had been turned off by the size and scope of the work. For us, 90 Brian Street turned into one of our best purchases ever.

Real-Life Example 9: The 1970s Dream House

The house at 94 Marcy Way was located in the Michael subdivision built in the late 1960s and early 1970s. The house would have been perfect—if the year had been 1970! Nothing in this house had been updated to modern standards.

It was obvious why this house wasn't selling. The seller (a bank) wouldn't invest the money in repairs and improvements to update the house. Similar houses for sale in the subdivision were also built in the late 1960s and early 1970s, but they'd been updated.

Obviously the seller wasn't going to have much success. Either the bank would need to invest in upgrades or adjust the Asking Price. After a bit of negotiating, we purchased the property at a substantial discount, made the required upgrades, and found a lease/purchaser in no time.

Are you surprised that the bank wasn't willing to do the upgrades to achieve maximum retail value on the sale of the property? As we discuss in detail in the next chapter for Golden Key 3, banks and lenders are in the business of lending money, not improving and managing the resale of properties. Some banks, as a matter of policy, don't upgrade at all. Others don't upgrade when the cost exceeds a certain amount. Still others make the decision on a case-by-case basis. These types of situations are perfect for the smart investor.

Real-Life Example 10: The Trashed House

Neither of us will ever forget 66 Ellen Lane in the Barry subdivision. After all, the flea bites we both got when we first viewed it are vivid reminders. The house was a perfect middle-income home and, from the outside, looked like every other house in the neighborhood. However, when we opened the door, we were immediately swarmed by fleas that had been preying on the family dog and cat. Their cousins, the ants, were dining on the leftover food thrown all over the house. This house had broken windows, lipstick painted on the walls—the list goes on.

This house on Ellen Lane is an extreme example of what homeowners often do when they are foreclosed on by the big, mean bank. Because the home is being taken away from them, they simply take out their frustration on the property or simply don't take care of it.

This is a big cosmetic mess for the bank. Some banks will have the house cleaned up and fixed up before showing it to prospective buyers. However, as we've discussed, it is amazing to us that many banks don't do this. They simply want to cut their losses and not invest any more money in the property or at least try to sell the home without further investment.

We contacted the bank about this house immediately after foreclosure. It was preparing to fix up the home and list it with an agent. We convinced the bank to do nothing and let us look at the house in its current condition. If we quickly purchased the home, the bank wouldn't need to lift a finger. The bank agreed and we bought the home within a couple of weeks after the foreclosure sale.

There are many properties like this: Properties that most people simply won't touch—whether they're looking to purchase and live in the house or invest in the house. Most people have a hard time finding the hidden beauty and they don't want the hassle (or simply don't like fleas). In this case, we purchased the home at a good discount, fixed it up, and lease/purchased it fairly quickly. The house on Ellen Lane turned out to be a real beauty of an investment.

WHAT A GOOD PROPERTY LOOKS LIKE TO US

Throughout this chapter, we've touched on what type of property we prefer when Buying Low. Today's good property for us is based on our many years of real estate investing experience, which we refer to as the *school of hard knocks,* as well as countless lessons we have learned from seminars, books, and other investors. We wish we had read a book like this when we started our real estate investing career. It probably would have helped us avoid many mistakes and given us significantly more confidence in our strategy. We hope that our book does this for you.

We've covered a lot of ground in this chapter. Accordingly, here is a summary of what a good property looks like to us.

- **Developed.** Big profits can be reaped from developing land or buying undeveloped land and flipping it or simply sitting on it. However, we prefer the more consistent, simpler, and less risky attributes associated with developed properties. The extra expenditure of time and effort has played a big role in why we have chosen not to develop a property yet.
- **Residential.** Commercial properties bring sound profits to those investors who understand them well (and usually invest in them full-time). However, residential properties are more plentiful with more good deals to choose from, usually less expensive if you make a mistake, and easier for most part-time investors like us.
- **Single family.** Multifamily properties are often cheaper to buy per square foot and may be easier to manage en masse. However, single-family properties usually require a smaller investment per property, which allows us to more easily diversify our portfolio. They also tend to work better for our Buy and Lease/Purchase investment strategy.
- **Houses.** Apartments, condominiums, and town homes can be wonderful investments. However, apartments often require you to buy the building and usually can only be rented, while condominiums tend to be higher risk in a down economy. Houses allow us to lease/purchase, they do well in a good economy, and they are more resilient during an economic downturn. Simply put, to many people, they help fulfill the American Dream.
- **Middle-income neighborhoods.** Low-income and high-income properties can generate big profits. However, we prefer middle-income houses for two primary reasons. First, there is a larger pool of these in most communities, which usually means more good deals. Second, our experience shows that most low-income people are not looking to buy and most high-income people don't need to "rent to buy."

However, there are many middle-income people looking to lease/purchase. Therefore, we've found that middle-income houses fit our lease/purchase model best.

- **Suburban.** There are many good investment opportunities in urban and rural communities. However, our experience shows that the largest number of single-family houses and available candidates for our lease/purchase formula are found in most suburban communities.

- **Three bedrooms, two bathrooms.** There are many wonderful houses to buy with a variety of features and characteristics. However, we either like to buy houses that most stable lease/purchasers will be looking for or houses that lack features that provide significant discount opportunities. Since we lease/purchase single-family houses, we tend to attract a lot of families with kids. They tend to need at least three bedrooms and two bathrooms. They also like garages, flat lots, and basements, so we look for these features when they are standard in the neighborhood. Again, if a particular neighborhood feature is missing, such as a garage, basement, or flat lot, we buy these properties only if we get a significant discount that we can more than offset with our lease/purchase terms and still turn a good profit.

- **Home residences.** Vacation properties can certainly be more fun. However, we choose to invest in properties we can keep an eye on, leverage our lease/purchase model, and cater to the American Dream. We use some of the profits from these houses to rent vacation properties all over the world.

- **Ugly and awful.** Mint-condition properties are clearly easier to deal with. However, ugly and awful properties often have the most profits locked up in them. We hope our stories helped you better understand why "ugly and awful" homes can be beautiful investments.

4

GOLDEN KEY 3—FIND GOOD PROPERTIES

There are many ways to find good properties to buy. Most models differ on key variables such as amount of available cash required, level of inherent risk, degree of contact with distressed sellers, and the amount of time required by the investor. In this chapter, we profile ten of the most common methods of finding good discount real estate. We also give you the inside story on how we arrived at our preferred method and secrets to using it successfully.

PREFORECLOSURES

One of the most talked-about ways of acquiring investment properties is purchasing preforeclosures. Many real estate gurus teach using preforeclosures to get big discounts on real estate.

A preforeclosure is a property purchased directly from a seller who has fallen behind in his or her payments to a financial institution. The property owner faces foreclosure of the home by the lender for not paying the mortgage.

Preforeclosures happen in two stages. The first stage begins when a property owner initially gets behind in paying the mortgage and lasts until the official notification of pending foreclosure. During this stage, if the property owner has equity in the property, he or she can catch up on payments owed and save the property, or sell it and take the equity gained from the sale. You can find stage one properties through sellers' ads, tips from friends, and real estate agents. Some investors place ads in the newspaper or other media advertising that "We buy houses fast" or "We pay good money for houses in distress and can act fast!"

The second stage happens the last month before foreclosure when a property owner is probably two to five months behind in mortgage payments. It's when the financial institution files for foreclosure and the property owner receives official notice of the pending foreclosure sale. The filing is a public record and (in many states) the foreclosing party is required to publish the pending foreclosure in the local or county newspaper for a certain number of weeks (often four weeks) before the foreclosure sale. Investors frequently review these publications for contact information. Some communities have a service that compiles these notices, publishes hard-copy lists, or displays them online for a fee. Investors obtain this information and usually contact owners facing foreclosure by mail or telephone. At this point, a property owner has little time to act (often fewer than four weeks) and will either be in denial about the pending foreclosure or will be ready to deal.

The number of preforeclosures has increased in the past few years. Sadly, this is largely due to the huge amount of debt many people carry today. Some foreclosures result from people having overpaid for their property. They weren't too concerned about that at the time of purchase because they anticipated their property would appreciate. But when people live beyond their means or speculate on property, many simply don't have ample cushions if their life events or speculations take a negative turn. Business failure, unexpected job loss, divorce, poor financial planning, and family illness are among the more common reasons people face foreclosure.

The best attribute of this method for finding good investment property is the abundant supply of homes available. This supply will probably continue to grow for years to come (especially during bad economic times) because of our ever-growing debt-laden and speculative society.

Another positive attribute is that preforeclosure properties don't take a lot of time and effort to find. After all, in stage one, desperate sellers may call *you* if you advertise in their community. And, in stage two, you'll find lots of properties listed among the pending foreclosures in the local newspaper and other foreclosure listings.

On the other hand, there are two primary negatives associated with this investment method. First, partly because so many books and seminars about preforeclosures tout this method, the field of investors going after preforeclosures is crowded in many communities. You'll run into many rookie investors fresh out of seminars that detail the wonders of purchasing preforeclosures. Because of their inexperience, they're likely to pay too much for these properties. By paying too much, they reduce the pool of available properties that have attractive discounts.

Second, dealing with preforeclosures means dealing with people (often families) caught in tough situations. For many, their lives are falling apart and they're distressed. Even if you deal with them honorably and respectfully, many will still view you as an opportunist or parasite. The emotional challenge of dealing with this can prove to be too difficult for many investors.

FORECLOSURE SALES

Foreclosure sales often attract investors looking for incredible deals. Some of the best examples yielding extraordinary profits revolve around foreclosure sales.

An **E**arly **E**xperience *with a* **P**reforeclosure

Early in our partnership, we planned to use this method as our primary vehicle to buy properties at a discount. We were among those starry-eyed investors who'd read about the fortunes awaiting us and had even attended seminars on the topic. However, the human element proved to be too much. We quickly abandoned this method; here's why.

Shortly after we started using the preforeclosure method, we found a family who was going to lose their home in two weeks. They knew they had to face reality after both the husband and wife lost their jobs within months of each other. When Andy visited their home, he was almost in tears as he walked through it. During his viewing, the little girl pulled him aside and pointed out the doggie window—the hole in the kitchen door cut out for the family dog to use.

We realized we were about to snatch this house—part of the history and lifeline of this family—and turn a profit from it. We simply didn't have the thick skin to repeat this activity. The "doggie window" house was the last preforeclosure we ever visited.

Fortunately, the husband landed a job within a week and the Veterans Administration came through with an emergency loan, so this family saved its "doggie window" home. But most endings aren't so happy. If you use this method to buy properties, be prepared to witness (and profit from) many similar sad stories.

As described above, if a property owner can't bring the mortgage current in the preforeclosure stage, then the property goes into foreclosure. This usually takes the form of an old-fashioned auction. On the first Tuesday of every month (in many states), the previous month's foreclosures get auctioned off to the highest bidder on the courthouse steps. Often, states require that successful bidders present certified funds for the full cash value of the winning bid price at the time of the auction or within 24 hours.

With foreclosures, investors don't have to deal with distressed sellers, which is an integral part of the preforeclosure method. Because the previous owner has already lost the property, the foreclosure method becomes simply a business transaction with investors bidding against others interested in buying the property.

However, a lot of surprising negatives come with foreclosures. For example, many have little equity in them as a result of creative borrowing in a low down-payment environment. Many creative loans made to homeowners for primary residences require ridiculously low down payments. Some programs structured to promote first-time homeownership don't even require a down payment. As a result, many properties, especially houses, go to foreclosure with little equity in the property. Consequently, not as many good foreclosure deals exist as you might expect.

In addition, many properties that go to foreclosure have been trashed by the owner as a form of revenge on the foreclosing entity. Others simply haven't been maintained due to lack of funds. Often it's hard to gain access inside these properties before the foreclosure sale because owners in dire financial straits stay in their properties to the very end. In fact, it's not uncommon for families to stay in the properties even after the foreclosure sale, remaining until the sheriff comes to evict them. Because of potentially hidden problems with the property, an "excellent deal" may actually be a nightmare. This is why most people who buy foreclosures on the courthouse steps are experienced investors.

There may also be hidden liens on the property that can't easily be found or assessed, such as tax liens, builders' liens, and other liens. Because foreclosures often happen within one month of public notice, properly researching potential hidden liens may prove challenging. During one of our attempts to purchase at a foreclosure sale, an attorney we knew did a quick search—incorrectly—and didn't find any liens. Fortunately, we didn't win the bid. After the auction, we found out it had a significant lien so we narrowly missed losing a substantial sum of money. Purchasing at foreclosure sales can be risky because key details can be missing or hard to find during the research phase.

Some companies purchase substantial numbers of investment properties at foreclosure sales. They often use attorneys to research each property they intend to bid on. If they happen to acquire a property with significant unexpected repairs or an unknown lien, they're able to offset occasional miscalculations with the volume of properties they purchase. Few investors can purchase in such a volume.

Research your state's laws concerning foreclosures. In some states, the previous property owner (who was foreclosed on) can purchase the property back from the new owner (the buyer at the foreclosure sale) during a preset period of time. Be prepared to deal with an emotional element attached to these situations.

Also keep this in mind: Because the foreclosure sale is an auction, you face the risk of getting caught up in the heat of the moment and paying more than you intended. It's best if you have a game plan and stick to it.

Yes, foreclosures can be profitable. However, the extreme risks associated with this method keep many investors away. If you're going to use it, we strongly encourage you to watch foreclosure sales ahead of time. We've viewed many of these sales and have attempted to buy a few times, but we've yet to use this method to buy a property.

POSTFORECLOSURES

Purchasing postforeclosure investment properties may not have all the glamour of the preforeclosure and foreclosure methods. However, they generally have less emotion and risk attached than the other two.

If the loan on a property isn't brought current during the preforeclosure stage and it isn't purchased at the foreclosure sale, then it goes back to the lender (the bank, mortgage company, or a person). As mentioned earlier, creative new loans that require low or no down payments to promote easy ownership have led to record numbers of foreclosures. Because they have so little equity, these properties aren't attractive to investors. Consequently, many go back to the lender.

If the lender is a financial institution (for example, a bank or mortgage company), then the property often goes to its real estate owned (REO), or postforeclosure, department. This department is entrusted with disposing of the foreclosed property. It's important to understand a key concept here: *Banks and mortgage companies are in the business of lending money, not managing a real estate portfolio.* Because they make their profits lending funds, having too many properties on their books in the REO department acts as a drain on their profits. Of course, lenders would like to maximize the resale value of their REO properties but they're often willing to discount them, especially when they've been on the books too long or when they have too many properties in their REO portfolios.

Lenders sell these properties in a variety of ways. Some sell directly to investors, others use real estate agents, and some do both. Small and regional financial institutions are normally the most accessible for investors, while larger financial institutions often require investors to deal with an agent. In either case, the process follows these steps.

Step 1: Call the Lender

The investor calls the main office of the national, regional, or local financial institution, explains that he or she is an investor and would like to talk to someone in the REO department. Depending on the size of the financial institution and the competence of the person you reach on the phone, it may take you multiple phone calls and a lot of persistence to get the right person.

Remember, financial institutions lend money. Therefore, receiving phone calls about buying their properties may be something many employees at the financial institution don't know about. For example, the receptionist or bank employee handling your call may not know how to assist you. Don't give up. Realize that their lack of knowledge doesn't indicate how many foreclosed properties a lender may have. Be patient. We've lost count of the number of times we've heard classic lines such as, "We don't do foreclosures."

Step 2: Introduce Yourself as an Investor

Once you connect with someone in the REO department, identify yourself as an investor in the community where you want to purchase properties or tell him or her you've been tracking a particular property. Ask the department's representative if you can work with him or her directly to buy properties and ask about the specific policy for dealing with REO properties. The representative may refer you to an agent who deals with disposing of these properties in your target community and/or may agree to add your name to a monthly e-mail distribution list of the institution's foreclosures and/or tell you to call each month to find out what properties are available.

Most of the larger financial institutions and some of the regional ones have real estate agents (called REO agents) they work with in each community. Among the top real estate agents in the community, REO agents often have worked hard to build a relationship with the financial institution. They can play a huge role in your success using the postforeclosure method. In many communities, a handful of REO agents control the vast number of postforeclosures. Therefore, finding and developing relationships with them can be critical.

Postforeclosure properties have a lot of attractive characteristics. First, there is a large pool of them. As previously mentioned, this has been fueled by the increasing numbers of foreclosures on properties with little or no equity.

Unlike preforeclosure properties, postforeclosures are owned predominantly by companies (banks and mortgage companies). This makes for a simple business transaction; the seller is not as

How to **F**ind **R**EO **A**gents
Here are three ways to find REO agents.

1. *Contact the financial institutions.* As discussed above, when you contact the financial institution, the lender may give you the names and contact information of REO agents the company works with in a target community. Simply call the agent and tell him or her that the bank referred you. This is a great way to gain immediate credibility with the REO agent.

2. *Network within your community.* As we began investing in our target community, we met a large number of top real estate agents. One day, we were at lunch with a top agent who didn't specialize in post-foreclosure properties but shared the names of several of these agents. We got busy calling them and introducing ourselves. Although we've picked up more names over the years, that one networking lunch proved to be golden.

3. *Look for signs.* Contact the agents listing these properties that have "Bank Owned" or "Foreclosure" on the real estate signs in front of the houses. Ask about these properties, and ask the agents if they commonly list other postforeclosure properties.

emotionally attached to the deal as an owner who is living at the property.

Unlike most foreclosures, postforeclosures are available for viewing and inspection. You can preview the property and determine repair and improvement costs.

Unlike most preforeclosures and foreclosures, you should have a lot more time between putting a contract on the house and closing on it, which gives you time to assess repairs and improvements and conduct a thorough title search. By doing this, you can eliminate the risk and expenses of dealing with hidden problems.

Postforeclosures also don't require the significant cash outlays of foreclosure sales and other investment methods. You typically have a reasonable amount of time to find a loan, such as 30 to 60 days.

Because most postforeclosures are owned by financial institutions, you may also have the opportunity to obtain in-house financing. After all, their business is lending money. This could simplify the purchase process for you while reducing your financing costs if the lender is willing to absorb the closing costs of its in-house loan.

Postforeclosures can also be an easy way to find good properties. Once you've identified and built relationships with the appropriate people in these financial institutions or their real estate agents, don't be surprised to receive phone calls or e-mails about new purchasing opportunities. Once you've established the key contacts in your community, it becomes easier to purchase subsequent properties. If you're investing in properties while still working a day job, this will be a huge benefit. It will help you maximize the growth potential of your portfolio by minimizing the time spent in the Buy Low phase of real estate investing. In fact, we have purchased the majority of our properties from just a handful of contacts.

Like everything else, no method is perfect. Probably the most significant negative associated with purchasing postforeclosures is the sometimes limited investor margin. Real estate agents generally market postforeclosures because this allows for maximum exposure of the properties to the retail market. It also creates the highest level of competition for the properties. You will, therefore, often be competing with other investors and retail buyers (people who would live in or use the property). Financial institutions must take into account the 6 to 7 percent they're paying in real estate commission. This can impact the lender's willingness to negotiate on the property.

For postforeclosures, profit margins of 10 to 20 percent are common. Therefore, if you want to make a killing in just a handful of real estate investments, postforeclosures alone may not be the right way for you to find good properties.

For us, postforeclosures are a big component of our Buy Low, Rent Smart, Sell High investment strategy. We've made significant amounts of money using this method, saved a lot of time by leveraging the relationships we've built, and realized profits that are dependable and consistent.

DISTRESSED SELLERS

Residential property is the best place to use this method. These homeowners are not facing foreclosure; they're in financial trouble and want to sell their properties to get their financial situation under control. Divorce, job loss, and illness are some of the most common reasons people find themselves in distressed situations and needing to raise cash quickly.

How do you find distressed sellers? The best way is to place newspaper ads and post signs offering to purchase homes quickly. These signs may read: "We Buy Homes" or "Cash for Your Home Now." Networking with divorce attorneys may also yield results.

Depending on how fast a distressed seller needs to sell and how quickly you can act, you may be able to get a considerable discount. Unlike preforeclosures, because the property owner isn't facing foreclosure, the urgency factor may be somewhat reduced. This means you may be able to base your offer on getting an investor loan rather than using cash. You'd also have time to do a thorough repair and improvement assessment, as well as a title search.

On the other hand, the cons with this method are identical to those for preforeclosures—the biggest one being the human element of dealing with people in dire situations. Yes, this method can be profitable but it often entails profiting from people in a bind.

REAL ESTATE AUCTIONS

Real estate auctions have become increasingly common in recent years. We've heard of incredible buys, and we've used this method ourselves.

Popular auction houses such as Hudson & Marshall regularly schedule real estate auctions in major metropolitan areas, although they're not limited to properties in that metropolitan area. For example, Hudson & Marshall holds regular auctions in Atlanta but the auction usually includes properties throughout the state of Georgia.

Most auctions resemble foreclosure sales, with the winning bidders required to pay in full within one or two business days of the auction. Some allow investors to purchase with financing as long as they bring proof of prequalification; others allow financing without requiring any up-front proof. Some auction houses guarantee there will be no title problems with the property.

To locate reputable auction houses in your area, start by networking with local real estate agents, joining a local real estate investment club, or meeting established real estate attorneys. You may also find auctions by checking the local newspaper's real estate section or searching the Internet.

Properties rarely go to auction as the owner's first choice of sales outlets. In fact, most properties going this route have already been listed with a real estate agent. They go to auction because the agent simply hasn't produced an offer the seller is willing to accept. After a period of time waiting for an acceptable offer, the seller simply wants to try another approach.

Because every auction house has its own set of rules, take time to familiarize yourself with the specific operating parameters of each before coming to bid. Most maintain a free mailing list and Web site that list houses scheduled for sale at an upcoming auction. Often, the present listing agent or the auction house provides access to the house before the auction date. If at all possible, preview the properties in advance of the auction to determine whether they meet your investment criteria.

When a seller notifies the listing agent of plans to sell the property at an auction, this often serves as a wake-up call to the agent that the seller isn't pleased with the results of the listing efforts. As a reaction, the agent may step up sales efforts in the weeks leading up to the auction and some properties scheduled for auction never make it there. They go under contract or get sold just before the auction.

Inexperienced real estate auction investors may not know about this last-minute sales push by the agents. They think every house publicized for sale at the auction will indeed be auctioned off. They then get frustrated when many of the houses they've spent time to assess aren't included. Does the auction house do this intentionally to draw more traffic to the auction? We don't have the answer. It makes sense for an auction house to want to draw traffic to the auction. It's also reasonable to assume that investors who show up and are disappointed to find their targeted properties already sold might consider bidding on another property or bidding higher on one of their other targeted properties simply because they're present and eager to bid. Beware of this.

Like investors who buy using the foreclosure method, some like the auction format in which you bid publicly and quickly against others. If you have enough self-control and willpower to handle the exhilaration at an auction environment, this method can be profitable and fun.

Real estate auctions can be a great way to buy discount properties, as well as an efficient use of your time. If the auction house carries a nice portfolio of properties, you can preview those that meet your investment criteria. You then simply come to the auction prepared to purchase these properties.

An auction also eliminates negotiating, an unavoidable step for most methods of buying real estate and one that not all investors enjoy. Instead of negotiating for weeks with a seller, you bid for a few minutes against other investors who want the same property. If you have the discipline to stop bidding at your Maximum Purchase Price (the top purchase price that still gives you an adequate Total Investor Discount, which is described in Golden

Key 4), you can walk away without the heartache commonly experienced in many time-consuming real estate negotiations.

On the other hand, procedures, policies, and experience may vary significantly from one auction house to another. So be careful when buying through auctions. Research them before showing up to their auctions and especially understand the contract terms to which you'd be committing yourself.

As mentioned above, some auction houses deal only with investors who can come up with 100 percent cash within a specified amount of time, generally 24 hours. This is similar to bidding on properties at a foreclosure sale. Obviously, if you don't have that type of cash readily available, then these particular auctions aren't for you.

Some auction houses don't operate in a professional manner. Because buying a property is substantially riskier than buying a low-ticket item like an antique table, be especially careful. If bidding on a big-ticket item makes you extremely nervous, you should probably not use real estate auctions to buy discount properties.

As you know, the auction process plays on people's emotions and desire to win. If you don't have a lot of self-discipline, an auction house may not be a good source for you to seek discount real estate. It's not low-risk bidding. This is not like bidding on a $1,000 designer chair. That's why you're wise to walk into an auction house with a plan (especially a Maximum Purchase Price) and feel confident you'll be able to resist straying from it.

This method can be quite profitable—and exciting. The "electricity" at some auctions can really draw you in. Before long, you get caught up in the excitement and want to leave with one of the "prizes" for your efforts and time invested. When we participate, we often come prepared to bid on several houses, with established Maximum Purchase Prices on each. We exert the utmost willpower to keep from exceeding that price because we know the process preys on the emotional energy in the room.

Remember, the main reason sellers use auctions to sell property is that they anticipate a higher return than they'd get with the listing agent. Even with the commission paid to the auction house, sellers generally get more money than if they discounted the property and kept it listed with their real estate agent. Some sellers have the auctioneers set a starting bid that's already above the previous net listing price (the old listing price minus the real estate commission they won't be paying). Understanding the seller's motivation to use an auction house may be helpful to install the discipline you need to successfully bid at an auction.

This is not our number one method for buying properties at a discount because our postforeclosure sources feed us plenty of leads on good properties. However, because we have had success with this method, we do employ it from time to time.

Don't Exceed the Maximum Purchase Price
We fondly remember our partnership's first auction. Scott had a scheduling conflict so Andy went by himself. The previous day, Scott had repeatedly warned Andy to keep his emotions in check and not to exceed the agreed-upon Maximum Purchase Price for each property he'd bid on. Andy still remembers that Scott's warnings were so strong, they kept echoing in his head during the auction. He purchased one of the five properties they'd researched, which was the last of approximately 30 properties auctioned off that night. Andy still remembers how frustrated he became as the first four properties sold for more than the Maximum Purchase Price we had established. However, Andy did not let his emotions get the better of him. You may not have Scott's strong words of caution ringing in your ears. However, be disciplined enough not to exceed the Maximum Purchase Price you identify for each property.

One final thought on auctions: Since the early 2000s, certain Internet auction houses have become popular. For example, we're told that many millions of dollars of real estate are bought and sold each year on eBay. We've never used the Internet to buy real estate but we've heard that it works from eBay experts such as Adam Ginsberg, who has a product called *How to Buy and Sell Real Estate on eBay.*

TAX LIENS AND TAX DEEDS

The basic premise behind the tax lien is that a county needs the revenue from taxes today to pay for the services the county offers to the residents of the county tomorrow. When a property owner becomes delinquent with his or her taxes, the county no longer has these funds to pay for the county services. Therefore, the county "auctions" the delinquent property owner's tax obligation in the form of a tax lien. We compare tax liens to stocks—without the risk of losing your entire investment. Generally, it's difficult to lose money on tax liens. This is because many states guarantee the principal and even a minimum return.

Because procedures vary by state and even by county in the bidding process, be sure to research the specific ones used in the states and counties you target. Many states have a minimum amount an investor is allowed to bid, so inquire about that. Once you acquire the lien, the initial property owner is usually given time (one to two years) to redeem the tax debt. If the lien is not redeemed by the property owner, the lien holder (the investor) can foreclose on the property and become its new owner.

With tax liens, in many cases, you don't acquire the physical property. If you don't have the stomach for dealing with selling properties and landlording headaches, this could be the perfect buying method. It's like investing in real estate on paper only. Additionally, with online tax lien auctions becoming more popular and opening up to nonresidents, you may be able to sit in your house or office and actively bid on these kinds of properties thousands of miles away.

A big misconception about tax lien properties is that they're mostly "crack houses," unusable tracts of vacant lots, and other properties in horrible condition that nobody wants. While many properties fall into these categories, plenty of desirable properties also have tax liens, often due to simple neglect. The owner can afford the taxes but just didn't pay by the due date. For example, wealthy owners might own their houses free and clear, so the taxes aren't conveniently paid from their mortgage's escrow accounts. They simply forget to pay their taxes without the aid and convenience of having an escrow account.

Many Americans with ample means don't mail their taxes by April 15 and also fail to request an extension within the appropriate time frame. No one really knows why people who have means forget to do this. However, enough do to add to the appeal of tax lien investing.

"Tax deed" states operate differently from "tax lien" states. Tax deed states actually sell the property for an amount in excess of the back taxes owed. If, for example, a property owner owes two years of back taxes at $4,000 each year on a $250,000 house, the bidding would begin at $8,000. While acquiring a $250,000 house for $8,000 is theoretically possible, it's not probable. Also, like foreclosure sales, many tax deed states require full payment shortly after the auction so the investor will need access to ample funds. This serves as an obstacle and will eliminate many potential investors in tax deed transactions.

It's our understanding that the best deals at tax deed sales are vacant lots. This is because it's much more likely that owners decide they no longer want to keep paying taxes on vacant lots than on properties with a structure, especially a house in which they live.

There are also some hybrid states, which are tax deed states that allow previous owners the right to reacquire their properties within a certain period of time. In a hybrid state, the previous owner has the right to purchase back the property from investors for the sale amount, administrative costs, and a penalty percentage that could reach up to 25 percent of the bid amount. While it may seem unlikely that previous owners will come up with these funds soon after not managing to pay the taxes, it is still a possibility.

Both tax liens and tax deeds offer an attractive potential return on investment while never actually taking possession of the property. In fact, it's more like investing in a stock or bond, hoping for the highest possible rate of return. However, unlike a stock or bond, tax liens and tax deeds usually allow you to minimize the risk of losing your investment because you should be purchasing these tax liens and tax deeds for less than the property is worth. Although you probably won't lose substantial amounts of money investing in tax liens and deeds, the bigger question is "How much profit can you really make this way?"

In addition, this form of acquiring properties is arguably among the most complicated methods. Be sure to do your homework before investing in tax liens and tax deeds. Their complex nature discourages a lot of inexperienced investors who don't have the time, expertise, and patience to learn the process.

If you make a mistake, you could end up with an unusable vacant lot or an undesirable property that costs more to manage and dispose of than you spent to acquire it. While many vacant lots are great deals, a vacant lot can come with problems. So be careful and understand the value of the property in its existing or improved condition. If you're not sure of what you're getting into, don't buy the tax lien or tax deed on the property.

Many institutional investors such as large banks are attracted to tax lien and tax deed investing. These institutional investors may come to sales and purchase hundreds and even thousands of these. This can be frustrating for the individual investor.

The elements of time and frustration can be additional negative factors. Assuming you're careful and want to preview every property you bid on, this approach can take large amounts of time. Many properties set to go to auction are believed to become current just before the sale. This means you may preview ten properties just before the sale, but only five or fewer are actually auctioned off. If an institutional investor comes in and buys all five of those properties, you've just spent a lot of time with nothing to show for it.

To date, we've not purchased a tax lien or tax deed. We're skeptical about the "easy wealth" available with tax liens and tax deeds that some investors promote. Rarely is any type of investment vehicle "easy." Every investment vehicle carries risk in the form of its potential return. If the return is minimal, why bother?

For more information, *Profit by Investing in Real Estate Tax Liens* by Larry Loftis offers a fairly easy-to-follow assessment of investing in tax liens and tax deeds. The author covers the differences between them and explains which states are lien states, deed states, and hybrid states.

POUND THE PAVEMENT

Many real estate investors don't use a sophisticated system to acquire real estate. They simply rely on that trusted old-fashioned formula: *hard work + hard work + hard work = results.*

We can't tell you how many books and newsletters we've read promoting the benefit of hard work and pounding the pavement. Many successful investors have made their fortunes using nothing more than this method.

One way to "pound the pavement" is to simply view and make many offers on houses listed for sale in your community. But because investors factor putting a big discount in their offer to purchase, many (if not most) of these offers don't get accepted. Some property owners, especially homeowners, may be offended by your "lowball" offers. You'll also probably run into some real estate agents that get upset because they feel you're wasting their time.

If you want to save some time, aggravation, and money, we have a suggestion: Put together a flyer or letter that introduces you as a real estate investor seeking to acquire properties and send this to people in your target market. For example, if you want to purchase a single-family property, the flyer or letter should go to any property you're interested in buying, including those with "For Sale by Owner" signs in their yard, properties listed by agents, and even houses that aren't yet on the market. Your flyer or letter could include an introduction (who you are and your objective), full contact information, key information points (such as "I can act quickly, I am prequalified/have cash financing, and I am fair"), and a brief overview of the benefits of working with you.

Writing an effective brief overview is important because people don't want to "give away" their property. If they view you as a shark preying on their anxiety over the pending sale of their property or as a nuisance, then you probably won't get a call from them.

Sample Introductory Letter

To: Homeowner in Pleasant Hills subdivision

"Hello, I'm Chloie Adkins, an investor seeking to acquire residential real estate. I am looking for win-win situations in which I can make a reasonable return on my investment and homeowners can sell their house in a quick and painless way. If you're considering selling your house now or soon, please consider me as an alternative to the regular sale-and-listing process.

What I offer makes life simpler for you because **you can avoid the following** by working with me:

- *Fix- up costs:* Most sellers spend hundreds or thousands of dollars fixing their houses and preparing them for sale.
- *Real estate commission:* If you use a real estate agent, you'd probably pay a 6 to 7 percent real estate commission that comes out of the sales price of your property.
- *Time to show the house:* You will either need to schedule times to show your house or schedule times to be away from your house while an agent shows it.
- *Negotiating and discounting:* You'll likely engage in negotiating with the buyer and end up discounting your sales price in the long run.

*S*ample *I*ntroductory *L*etter *(continued)*

- *Double mortgage costs:* There is often a time overlap between when you sell your old house and when you buy your new house. Many homeowners aren't able to match this up and end up paying a mortgage on two residences for a time while only living in one.
- *Stress:* Many houses sit on the market for weeks or even months until they get a contract. This can be stressful and may also lead to a reduction in the sales price.

All of the above can easily add up to 10 percent or more of the sales price. Plus, saving time and reducing stress should have significant value to you.

My approach is simple. I come in and determine the Fair Market Value of the house, then I make an offer, seeking a fair investor discount of 10 to 20 percent (depending on particular aspects of your house). You'll have no multiple strangers come into your house, no extensive marketing period, and no hassle. The best part is I'm flexible on setting the purchase date, so I can time it to match the exact date when you want to vacate the property.

If this approach sounds reasonable and beneficial, please call me at (123) 456-7890. I'm happy to provide references who will confirm that I can take action quickly and I deal in a fair way. You'll find that I'm known for achieving win-win outcomes for both the buyer and seller. Thanks for your time.

Sincerely,

Chloie Adkins
ca@bellsouth.net
(123) 456-7890

When the property owner follows up with you, you assess the Fair Market Value of the house, determine your investor discount, and make an offer. Allow yourself a bit of wiggle room in your offer for some negotiation. (We discuss determining the right offer price, making the offer, and negotiating in Golden Keys 4, 5, and 6.)

Pound the pavement and make a lot of offers and you'll probably acquire some properties at a discount. Sellers may not accept your offer initially but may come back months later after getting frustrated with other sales methods.

This may be the best method if you're a beginning investor with limited finances. In addition, some private sellers may be in a position to offer financing, which can minimize your net cash outlay when acquiring their property. Of course, this may come with a price because they may demand a higher sales price in exchange for favorable financing terms. Whatever you do, be careful not to exceed your Maximum Purchase Price (the top price with an appropriate investor discount). Otherwise, you may buy properties that have good financial terms but insufficient profits.

On the other hand, this method can yield the worst return on time and effort compared to most other methods, especially when you don't prequalify properties with a flyer or letter. If you're simply previewing properties and making a lot of offers, most owners won't accept your offer. Not everyone can afford such a large time investment and certainly not everyone has the patience to hear "no's" time after time. Additionally, the flyer or letter approach simply may not provide many leads.

This method also exposes you to the human element. These owners, especially homeowners, likely have an emotional attachment to their property and may view you skeptically as preying on their valuable possession. Additionally, real estate agents often don't appreciate having to deal with perceived "lowball" offers.

A few words of caution: If you approach a property owner whose property is listed with an agent, you obviously know they want to sell it. However, if you tender an offer or even discuss price during the period the seller is listing the house with an agent, most listing agreements will require the seller to pay a real estate commission. This holds true even if the property gets sold

A *Personal* **P**ound*-the-***P**avement **E**xperience

Andy once used the pound-the-pavement method to find his primary residence. He wanted to live in a particular section of Atlanta and knew exactly what type of property he would buy. Andy drove around and introduced himself to homeowners who were listing their houses for sale. For those using a real estate agent, he told them to call if their listing agreement expired and they weren't making progress selling their house.

The first house he targeted went under contract two weeks before the listing agreement expired. However, he got a contract on the second house he targeted just days after the homeowner's listing agreement expired. It became Andy's primary residence for more than ten years. The seller gave Andy the full benefit of the 6 percent real estate commission the seller didn't have to pay, plus another 4 to 5 percent for simple ease of transaction. As a bonus, the seller had reduced the sales price on the property during the final three weeks of the listing agreement. All in all, not a bad deal. Even better, Andy achieved this deal in one of the hottest sections of Atlanta.

after the listing agreement expires. One way to prevent misunderstandings is to tell the property owner that you're interested but don't want to discuss the property or make an offer while the property is still listed. Give the property owner your card or introductory letter, and ask to be contacted after the listing agreement expires. Please note that even if you are very careful, some listing agents still may claim they deserve a commission simply because you viewed the property while it was listed with them. This obviously can impact the prospective purchase.

The pound-the-pavement method is the ultimate numbers game and certainly not very technical. As long as you can properly assess the market value of the properties you're looking at, all you'll need are funds, time, patience, and a full tank of gas.

Although this method can lead to big profits, we don't use this method. The tremendous amount of time required and the significant human element associated with it simply don't appeal to us.

CORPORATE RELOCATIONS

Large corporations seem to be constantly moving their employees around the country. Some companies even move their entire offices. In either case, the employee of the company or the company itself may have a property that needs to be sold.

Today, when employees (especially executives) are transferred, the company often takes responsibility for selling the transferring employee's house. In this situation—or if the company is trying to sell a building—it often enlists the aid of a corporate relocation real estate agent.

The process of positioning yourself to purchase corporate relocation properties is identical to postforeclosures with one modification: You may need to directly contact companies that aren't in the business of real estate. If you choose to contact a company to buy its employees' houses, we recommend starting with the human resources department. If you're looking to buy commercial real estate from a company, then you probably want to contact its real estate department.

The best time to contact a company directly is when you become aware of a significant, one-time transfer of employees. For example, you might see a newspaper article that reads, "Marie Enterprises, located in North Brunswick, New Jersey, announces plans to transfer its corporate headquarters to Palmetto, Florida. President Scott Marie is an avid sailor and has grown tired of living in the cold Northeast . . . so he's moving the entire company. Of the middle and senior executives, 50 percent are expected to leave the company and 50 percent are expected to transfer to Florida. Scott Marie's top executives, Diana, David, Danielle, and Dennis, will be joining him in Florida." This means a significant number of Marie Enterprises families will be moving out of the North Brunswick area.

If you live in or near North Brunswick, you'd immediately contact Marie Enterprises to locate the person or department (usually HR) managing the terms and affairs of the transferring executives. When dealing with a significant corporate transfer, don't be surprised if a special team has been formed to deal with the issues of the transferees. In either case, they can deal directly with you or put you in touch with their real estate agents.

The best characteristic about corporate relocations is that, like postforeclosures, it leverages strong relationships with real estate agents. Just as you find specific agents with a significant number of REO properties in their portfolios, you'll also find a handful of specific agents who are corporate relocation specialists. Follow the steps suggested for finding agents for postforeclosures and network until you develop strong relationships with some of these agents. Once you have the relationships in place, don't be surprised to see them bring deals your way.

The negative characteristics of this approach are similar to those for postforeclosures. If your community is large enough to have specific agents who handle a volume of corporate relocations, they're probably well networked among the investor community. Therefore, you'll probably face competition for buying discounted properties and you may be challenged to secure adequate investor discount.

Be aware of one significant negative difference compared to postforeclosures. Every community has foreclosures, so it may be easier to find these REO agents. On the other hand, significant corporate relocations primarily happen in larger cities, so it's likely harder to locate corporate relocation agents in smaller cities in which corporate relocations happen less frequently and affect fewer properties.

Corporate relocations can be a wonderful source of investment property. Read the newspapers, follow what the major companies are doing in your area, and be ready. If you're able to locate and build a relationship with an agent who specializes in corporate relocations, this can be one of the easiest ways to buy discounted real estate.

ESTATE SALES

In warmer states popular among retirees—Arizona, California, Florida, Nevada, and Texas—we've come across investors who've put a creative spin on "willed" property. We understand that some of these investors have made big profits from buying properties from heirs of people recently deceased. This buying method is often referred to as buying at an estate sale.

These investors scan the obituaries in the local paper, then do research to determine whether the deceased person owned his or her property. The investors track down the heirs of the deceased. Sometimes they also network among estate attorneys who are privy to much of this information. Some attorneys pass on the investor's contact information to the heirs while others aren't as inclined to work with investors.

Many heirs, especially close family members, feel distressed about the passing of their loved one. The absolute last thing they want to deal with is a time-consuming and involved business issue, especially crossing state lines. With this method, you can make a quick offer to the heirs and ask for a reasonable discount on buying their property. If it all lines up, everyone wins: You get a house at a reasonable discount; heirs avoid the hassle and emotional distress of fixing up, listing, and marketing the property of a dear, departed loved one.

How to Contact Heirs about Buying Properties of a Loved One

Your contact with the heirs might go something like this: "Hello, I'm Richard Martin and I'm a local real estate investor based in Miami Beach, Florida. I'm sorry to hear about the passing of your mother, Mrs. Jones. I try to seek a win-win situation with out-of-town people in your position. If you grant me access to the property, I will have a fair offer with a reasonable investor discount to you within one week."

Some investors promise heirs they'll give the full tax value of the property. This may sound like a fair deal. However, in many counties and states, the published tax values don't represent the Fair Market Value of the properties. In fact, it's not uncommon for the tax value to be 60 to 70 percent of the property's actual Fair Market Value. We don't believe in taking advantage of people, so we wouldn't use this approach unless we knew the tax values represented the Fair Market Values of the properties.

When a property is inherited, the heir commonly experiences grief and other emotional distress. Even though the departed intended to pass on the asset, some heirs feel guilty when profiting at the expense of a deceased loved one. Given all these feelings, it's easy to understand why many who are willed real estate want to sell the property as quickly as possible, even when it means sacrificing some of its value.

Some heirs may choose to simply sell all of the deceased person's belongings in an estate sale auction. In this case, the procedures for investors are similar to the procedures for other auctions described earlier. Estate sale auctions aren't difficult to find. Most are advertised in local papers and on Web sites.

Because many heirs are simply more interested in cleaning up the estate (selling off its assets) than profiting from the death of a loved one, good discounts may be available. Also, many retirees own their houses outright. With no loan attached to the property, the investor may be able to secure a degree of owner financing from the family or friend who has inherited the property. Accordingly, this buying method may be even more attractive to the cash-strapped investor.

On the other hand, a large number of retirees may not reside in your state, so the supply of properties and the market for this method may be limited. Also, it may feel awkward to track down the heirs of the recently deceased person and seemingly benefit from their grief. The human element of dealing with grieving heirs can be too much for many investors.

We've never tried this method, but we know one particular investor in Florida who has done well buying houses this way. We're told that a key aspect to this method is speed: it's critical to make contact with heirs quickly while emotions are fresh. If you wait too long, the pain of the loss and the emotional roller coaster may have eased up and your offer may no longer seem attractive to them. As long as you can deal with contacting family and friends soon after the loss of a loved one, this can be a profitable and not overly technical method of acquiring discount real estate.

BULK INSTITUTIONAL PURCHASING

This method of finding good investment properties offers some of the biggest profits. Bulk institutional purchasing works well for investors with access to large amounts of cash or credit so they can buy large numbers of properties in bulk and get steep discounts.

To get started, approach the REO (or postforeclosure) department of a large or regional financial institution (bank, mortgage company, etc.) that regularly has foreclosures. Introduce yourself to the REO manager responsible for the properties in your target community.

As an example, let's assume you're targeting foreclosures in the greater St. Louis, Missouri, area and Lily Rose is the REO manager in charge. You offer 60 cents on the appraised dollar to immediately acquire up to ten properties, sight unseen, in St. Louis. Lily Rose has too many properties in the bank's portfolio and accepts your offer. It's an easy way to purchase ten properties from the bank's portfolio.

If you're purchasing properties in bulk, you usually can't be highly specific about the neighborhoods and price range of the properties. In effect, you acquire properties for investor discount alone, with little regard to the specific attributes of each individual neighborhood and property.

Today, with the large numbers of foreclosures, banks and mortgage companies that make their livelihood lending money often find themselves with portfolios of hundreds of properties they need to move off their books. Within these banks and mortgage companies, REO managers have to market these properties. It's not uncommon for these companies to tell their REO managers to reduce the bank's portfolio quickly. This is when the bulk institutional investor can make a killing.

The bulk institutional investors are attractive to the bank because they represent a means of unloading a lot of property at one time with no real estate commission and with minimal holding costs. It's unlikely you'd be able to do this if you want to purchase just two or three properties, but you can try. Generally, you'd need to offer to purchase a significant number of properties to attract the attention and interest of REO managers.

Purchasing multiple properties at any one time can be lucrative. If you have the means to do this, you can better position yourself for bigger investor discounts, which generally translates into bigger profits.

The main negative characteristic is that you'll need lots of cash or a huge line of credit. Not only will you need the funds to acquire multiple properties, you'll need the funds to complete the necessary repairs and improvements to each property. You'll also need the funds to cover the holding costs until the properties are sold, rented, or lease/purchased.

If available cash isn't a problem, you'll probably face two significant issues. The first is the need for multiple contractors to repair and improve the multiple properties in a given time. If you acquire five or ten properties at the same time that all need some repairs and improvements, you may need a large team of contractors to handle the volume of work. One option is to let properties sit until your trusted one or two contractors are available to work on them, but that adds to your holding costs.

The second issue is the need for a strategy to sell, rent, or lease/purchase all these properties that have different Fair Market Values and are located in different areas. This can become complex due to the wide variety of properties you might acquire. Perhaps your strategy will call for you to rent the low-income properties, market the middle-income properties using the Buy Low, Rent Smart, Sell High lease/purchase program, and flip the high-income properties for immediate gain. The point is that if you acquire properties in bulk, you may have to develop and implement different investment strategies at the same time.

Few beginning investors have the means to purchase in such quantities. However, if you aspire to be a full-time real estate investor, being in a position to purchase properties in bulk is a wonderful goal. On the other hand, if you're starting out and have ample financial resources to purchase in large quantities, we highly recommend you begin purchasing in smaller quantities until you get experienced at executing any of the investment strategies.

COLLECTING DATA ON GOOD PROPERTIES

What do you do when you find a good property? How do you determine whether it's an appropriate property to buy?

First, we'll assume the property fits your chosen investment strategy and is the type of good property you want. With that in place, the rest of the Buy Even Lower system is about properly analyzing the correct price of the property as an investment (the Maximum Purchase Price) and figuring out the best way to procure it at or below this price. (We detail these steps in Golden Keys 4, 5, and 6.)

However, there is an important step to finding good properties before analyzing and procuring them: basic data collection. Doing this confirms that the property is, in fact, a good property and worthy of your time and effort.

Basic data collection begins as soon as you receive a lead on a potentially good property. First, simply collect the address and particulars such as number of bedrooms, bathrooms, sales price, and any other particulars associated with the property (known problems, repairs needed, the community, etc.). You can usually get this over the phone from a real estate agent, off a Web site listing homes for sale, and so on.

Next, you collect data when you preview the property. If your selected strategy doesn't offer access to the *interior* of the property, we encourage you to actually go to the property and view its *exterior* before making any offer. When at the property, collect data on all the particulars you can observe. Take notes on the neighborhood, the size of the lot, and any problems you see (for example: bad roof, paint job needed, steep hill, etc.). If you can get inside the property, walk into each room and note the different rooms in the property as well as particular features and problems you see (for example: repairs needed, strange layouts, etc.). When you leave the property, also drive around the surrounding vicinity. Get a feel for the neighborhood. Capture data on similar properties for sale, for rent, and for lease/purchase. Is this property larger or smaller than most others? Does the community look stable or run down?

This initial basic data collection will help you decide whether this property is potentially good as an investment for you. Do the specifications match everything that was advertised or was it missing a bedroom, bathroom, or some other feature? Does the property need more work than you want to put into it? Does it look overpriced compared to similar properties for sale in the vicinity? If this property passes this initial test, then you will proceed to Golden Key 4, calculating the Maximum Purchase Price for the property.

Some investors simply take notes on a clean sheet of paper every time they collect the basic data. However, we recommend you use a checklist or form to systematically collect the data so you don't miss anything. You especially want to avoid doing your later analysis with incomplete data and also avoid a second drive to the property to collect more data.

Sample Potential Investment Property Form for Houses
You can modify this example for commercial properties, multiplexes, or any other type of potential real estate investment you are considering. You can also download a free editable copy of this checklist at *www.RegularRiches.com/checklist*.

Date Property Seen ____/____/____   BR ___ BA ___ GAR ___
Address _____
Asking Price _____
Probable Sales Price (fixed up) _____
Prob. Rent _____
Agent/Seller _____
Phone _____
Age _____ yrs.   Neighborhood _____
  1 or 2 story _____
  Driveway _____

Exterior: Roof _____ Landscape _____ Paint _____
  Trees _____ Front Yard _____ Back Yard _____
  Fenced _____ Porch _____ Patio _____
  Deck _____ Shed _____ Other _____

Den: _____ Fireplace _____ Walls _____
  Carpet _____ Ceiling _____ Size _____
  OH Light _____ Ceiling Fan _____ Other _____

Dining Room: Attached _____ Walls _____ Carpet _____
  Ceiling _____ Size_____ OH Light _____
  Ceiling Fan _____ Other _____

Kitchen: Size _____ Walls _____ Floor _____
  Stove/Dish./Fridge _____ Pantry _____ Cabinets _____
  Ceiling _____ Other _____

Garage: Size _____ Opener _____ Shelves _____
  Other _____

Hallway: Walls _____ Carpet _____
  Linen Closet _____ Other _____

Laundry Room: Location _____ Size _____
  Other _____

Master Bedroom: Size _____ Walls _____

    Carpet _____ Ceiling _____

1st Bedroom: Size _____ Walls _____ Carpet _____

    Ceiling_____ Closet_____ OH Light _____

    Ceiling Fan _____ Other _____

2nd Bedroom: Size _____ Walls _____ Carpet _____

    Ceiling _____ Closet _____ OH Light _____

    Ceiling Fan _____ Other _____

Master Bath: Size _____ Walls _____ Floor _____

    Pressure _____ Other _____

Hall Bath: Size _____ Walls _____ Floor _____

    Pressure _____ Other _____

Rentals and Lease/Purchases in Neighborhood

Address_____ Phone _____

    BR/BA/GAR _____ Rent _____

    Sec. Dep./Option $ _____

Address_____ Phone _____

    BR/BA/GAR _____ Rent _____

    Sec. Dep./Option $ _____

Address_____ Phone _____

    BR/BA/GAR _____ Rent _____

    Sec. Dep./Option $ _____

For Sale in Neighborhood

Address_____ Phone _____

    BR/BA/GAR _____ Price _____

Address_____ Phone _____

    BR/BA/GAR _____ Price _____

Address_____ Phone _____

    BR/BA/GAR_____ Price _____

MORE ON HOW WE FIND GOOD PROPERTIES

One key component of our success is that we selected an investment method, studied it, and used it over and over again. We haven't spread ourselves too thin. Instead, we chose to learn a method and perfect it. Now, we can execute it blindfolded.

We suggest the same to you. Regardless of the way you choose to find good properties, choose one or two preferred methods, practice them, and perfect them. You'll find that your proficiency and confidence will grow with each purchase and your profits should grow in proportion.

We've chosen to focus on and perfect postforeclosure (REO) properties as a way of finding discounted real estate. We like the large pool of properties available and prefer to deal with financial institutions rather than individuals emotionally attached to their properties. We can take an appropriate amount of time to thoroughly examine these properties and nurture ongoing relationships with REO professionals in the relatively small amount of time this method requires. Carefully read the examples and suggestions in this section. They'll explain in detail why we prefer the postforeclosure method and how you can better use it for yourself.

Work Directly with the Financial Institution

In this real-life story, we called an out-of-town bank to inquire about a postforeclosure on Bertram Drive. We located the bank's REO manager and identified ourselves as local investors. The REO manager was polite but explained that the bank always worked with real estate agents. He said the bank insisted on having an agent involved, especially when the foreclosed properties were located out of state.

We indicated we understood this policy. We then explained to the REO manager that many wholesale investors seek more than 30 percent below market value for REO properties. Our system lets us operate profitably at an investor discount of approximately 15 percent below market. If we could work out a compromise on this house, we'd need only an additional discount of 7 to 8 percent above a standard real estate commission to make this purchase work for us. Our offer would be reasonable and realistic.

This bank regularly foreclosed on a number of properties in the area. Not surprisingly, the bank and the local REO real estate agent used by the bank were no strangers to each other. We suggested that the REO agent perform a limited role in the transaction in exchange for a reduced commission. This would apply only in the event that we could purchase the property on Bertram Drive quickly.

In this situation, the REO agent would need to activate the utilities, allow us access, and provide the bank with a report on the property's condition and estimated value. For this service, the bank agreed to a commission of 1 percent (rather than 6 percent).

We thought our offer was fair. After some minor negotiations, we reached a win-win agreement. We bought a great property at 15 percent below market, the bank took the property off its books quickly (likely for the amount it would have secured using full real estate agent services), and the real estate agent made a few thousand dollars for just a few hours of work. We all came out ahead.

In our opinion, most investors who call the bank's REO managers stop when they are told about the financial institution's policy of not working directly with investors. We take great care with how we present our suggestions because we'd never tell others how to do their jobs. We're sometimes able to succeed because we establish a means to maintain the integrity of the bank's existing policy and its relationships with its real estate agents, while still allowing us to deal with the bank directly.

Finding Our First Investment Home Together

When we first started investing together, our strategy looked different from how it does today. In the beginning, we sought to purchase preforeclosure properties directly from distressed sellers, then flip the properties shortly after completing the necessary repairs and upgrades. To find available preforeclosures, we perused lists in county and local newspapers and subscribed to a foreclosure report. We learned that many communities in Georgia sold hard-copy and online lists of pending foreclosure properties.

In one of our early transactions, we honed in on a house on Addison Lane in the Olivia subdivision. Unfortunately, we couldn't purchase it before it went to foreclosure but, in the research process, we identified a number of key factors. We identified the approximate value of the home, the bank that carried the note and was initiating the foreclosure, the amount of the loan, and the original loan date. We estimated that the remaining balance of the loan was 90 to 95 percent of the Fair Market Value of the home. This information helped us estimate that the property had roughly 15 to 20 percent equity (we assumed a 10 percent down payment).

The owners couldn't sell the home to us or any other investors because they didn't become realistic about their situation until it was too late. Consequently, on the first Tuesday of the next month, the house on Addison Lane was no longer a preforeclosure and went up for auction on the courthouse steps as a foreclosure.

Our next step was simple. We didn't have the cash to purchase the property at the time of the foreclosure. However, we checked the county records and learned that the house didn't sell at the foreclosure sale. The bank had taken it back, putting it into postforeclosure.

Days after the foreclosure sale, we called the bank's main office and asked for the postforeclosure department. Our query landed on the desk of the REO manager, Austin Watson. We identified ourselves to Mr. Watson as investors and explained that we'd been following this property through the foreclosure process. We told him that, if he'd allow us access to the property to assess the condition, we would have an offer on his desk within a few business days. By working with a buyer like us at this stage, we explained, his bank would save the hassle of rehabbing the property and minimize holding costs, plus avoid paying a real estate commission. Mr. Watson agreed to give us access and time.

After minimal negotiations, we purchased the property on Addison Lane for about 15 percent below market. For Mr. Watson and the bank, the sale was a no-brainer because it took the property off the bank's books within 30 days while avoiding a 6 percent commission.

A word of caution: It's not always this easy to work with banks directly. Many large banks have a number of levels to climb before you can get to the right decision maker. Some banks have well-established policies dictating use of specific real estate agents for disposal of REO properties and won't talk to investors directly. However, keep in mind that bank policies can be negotiable. Do your best to show how the bank can come out ahead by working with you.

Finding Good REO Agents and REO Managers

One question we're asked frequently is how to find real estate owned (REO) real estate agents who have portfolios of foreclosure properties as well as REO managers in financial institutions. The following tips help you find these key professionals.

First, as we mentioned earlier, start by locating REO agents in your target investment community. Drive the neighborhoods in your target community and look for signs in front of houses for sale that read "Bank Owned" or "Foreclosure." REO agents add these phrases to attract more interest from their customers: buyers seeking discounts. You can also pick up the phone book or surf the Internet to identify real estate companies in your target community to contact.

To find REO managers, you may choose to ask an REO agent for some names. You can also use the phonebook and Internet to identify REO managers in banks and mortgage companies.

> **C**ontacting **R**eal **E**state **C**ompanies *to* **F**ind **R**EO **A**gents
> When you call a real estate company to find REO agents, your query can sound something like this: "Hello, I'm a real estate investor. May I please speak with the broker in charge of the office (you may already know this person's name based on the name of the company, for example Dylan Jack Real Estate Brokerage). "Mr. Jack, I'm Caroline Investor and I focus my efforts on purchasing postforeclosure properties. Does your real estate company list any foreclosed properties?" If the broker says yes, set up a meeting and introduce yourself and ask about properties this real estate company has in the price range on which you focus. If the broker says no, ask if he or she knows agents in the area who deal in foreclosed properties.

When making contact, identify yourself as an investor focusing on a particular community such as Chicago, Illinois. Ask for the REO department first, then the REO manager in charge of properties in the Chicago area. Ask whether the bank's representatives work with investors directly. If the answer is yes, ask for lists of current properties as well as procedures for working with the bank or mortgage company. If the REO manager says the bank doesn't work with investors directly, as we described earlier, simply ask for the names of the agents they use in the area. Although a bank may have an official policy to work only with REO agents, we're still sometimes able to buy directly from them. Asking never hurts. You may present a deal to the REO manager and the bank that is simply too good to pass up, saving the bank real estate agent commissions and other costs associated with holding the property.

Another way to find REO agents and REO managers is to ask other investors. On the one hand, many might not be willing to share their secret sources of real estate investments. On the other hand, some know their sources have substantially more properties than they can handle alone, and others are willing to help out people they consider friends. Plus, some investors aren't currently purchasing properties or simply want to earn brownie points with their sources by referring another investor to them.

Once you find good REO agents and managers, treat them like gold. Appreciate them appropriately with verbal thanks, gifts, lunches, and other creative, reasonable ways to build those relationships.

Be Patient with REO Agents and Managers

When dealing with REO agents and managers, be patient—sometimes very patient. Remember that the people you deal with to buy the property usually don't have an emotional attachment to it (they never lived or worked in it) and don't have their own money tied up in it. The REO agents and managers simply work for the financial institution that owns the property. For example, sometimes they may not return your calls on a timely basis. Sure, they're motivated to sell properties. However, they surely have other responsibilities. Don't get frustrated with these people. Be patient.

Your patience will pay off when the bank's executives tell the REO agents it's time to move certain properties off their books. This can happen at the end of the month, end of the quarter, end of the year, or any other day of the year. The point is, if you stay in contact with the REO agents and managers and remain patient, you never know when you will get that call: "We're ready to sell the property based on your last offer." Most of our postforeclosure purchases take more than a month to put under contract and some properties took several months to come through. Therefore, we've learned time and again that the old saying is true: patience is a virtue.

Developing REO Agent and REO Manager Relationships

Over the years, we've purchased the majority of our properties from just a handful of sources. This demonstrates that when you develop a relationship with a key REO agent or manager, it becomes easy to do repetitive deals. That's why it's important to handle your initial contact with any REO agent or manager with care and foresight. Always do your best to make a good first impression and never stop making good impressions. Be respectful, courteous, and professional. That's how you separate yourself from the many investors regularly calling these people. If you make a poor impression, you may eliminate a key resource or fail to distinguish yourself from the many other investors calling the same key sources.

As we touched on earlier, it's important to show appreciation for your key REO agents and managers. For example, in the mid-1990s, we purchased a number of properties from REO agent Marcy Falkof. Marcy loves fine dining. To show our thanks, every year in December we invited Marcy to lunch at the finest steakhouse in Atlanta. There was no hiding the pleasure on her face when we came together for our annual appreciation lunches. We've developed a strong relationship with her over the years and believe these annual lunches have played an important role. In fact, chatting at one of these lunches, we were surprised to learn from Marcy that few of her other investors showed similar gratitude. Even though we believed we were relatively small potatoes to her business, she clearly thought highly of us.

Similarly, we show thanks to other key sources by giving gift certificates to department stores, restaurants, and movies. For property sources we've contacted but haven't done much or any business with, we might send a card or $25 gift certificate. A note of caution: Some financial institutions may have special rules prohibiting the acceptance of gifts or have a maximum value for a gift, such as $25. Do your best to show thanks to your key sources without creating an awkward situation for them. Simply tell them

Making a Good Impression

Brian Denny was a well-respected REO real estate agent in our community. We had met him but never worked with him to purchase a property. We knew he represented a number of larger banks and believed that building a solid relationship with him would benefit us in the future.

We wanted to buy a property on Troy Lane in the Seth subdivision that Brian had listed. We had set our Maximum Purchase Price (the maximum price we would pay for the property, allowing for an investor discount, as well as repairs and improvements) at $150,000. The negotiation process took over three weeks. As it played out, we felt comfortable that our relationship with Brian was building and that he appreciated our professionalism and style in the negotiations. However, toward the end of the negotiation process, it became apparent that the final purchase price would exceed our Maximum Purchase Price by a few thousand dollars.

In Chapter 7 of *Buy Low, Rent Smart, Sell High* and for Golden Key 4 in this book, we make a point about not exceeding your Maximum Purchase Price, but we made an exception for the house on Troy Lane. Why did we stray from our rule? Because we would only exceed our Maximum Purchase Price by a few thousand dollars, and we believed we could make up a portion of our Buy Even Lower profit with a healthy Rent Smart return. Finally, and most important, we had already invested time and energy establishing ourselves with Brian; we were hungry to put ourselves on the map with him, a key REO agent. Because we were developing a relationship of mutual respect, we needed to be seen high on his radar screen.

After purchasing this house from Brian, we bought many more properties through him either at or below our established Maximum Purchase Prices. Today, our relationship with Brian continues to be strong and profitable. Yes, it's essential to follow your own guidelines such as your firm Maximum Purchase Price. However, developing a relationship with a key REO agent can make a significant difference to building your business. Therefore, you may need to invest money and time to develop and nurture these relationships.

how much you appreciate them and send appropriate gifts. If they can't accept them, they'll return them. In either instance, they'll know you appreciate them. (If you do encounter key contacts to whom you want to show thanks but they refuse a gift from you, you may want to find out which charity they favor and make a donation in their honor.)

We suggest you track what gifts you give from year to year to establish consistency. For example, if a key REO agent produced an average of one good property a year for us during the first five years, then increased to an average of three properties a year, we would consider increasing the amount of value for our annual holiday gift.

You might view these gifts as *costs* to your business. Instead, we recommend you look at them as *investments*. We've never been frivolous with our money, yet our gifts, cards, and thank-you lunches have all proven to play a role in building valuable relationships with our key REO agents and managers.

Maintaining Credibility with REO Agents and Managers

The following story illustrates how we stuck to our Maximum Purchase Price and maintained our credibility along the way.

Fixed up, the home at 34 Sebastien Street was probably worth $325,000. It needed about $20,000 in repairs and the Asking Price was $289,000. Our Maximum Purchase Price was $255,000. The home was listed with one of our key REO agents, Deborah Bernard, who was representing ABC Bank, and John Swanson, a key REO bank manager.

The home at 34 Sebastien Street was the first one built in the subdivision, located close to the main street. This large, five-bedroom home was offered for sale in the middle of the summer. We anticipated Ms. Bernard would have difficulty selling this house because families (particularly larger families) prefer to move in the late spring and early summer to work around the school year. It was midsummer already and the bank was just weeks away from the end of the spring/summer selling season. We also thought that the proximity to the main street would eliminate families with younger children; parents would never be comfortable with a home so close to a main road. Due to these facts and other minor issues, we expected the seller would have difficulty selling this home.

When we offered $240,000, the seller barely budged from the Asking Price. There were a couple of rounds of negotiations, then we stopped at our Maximum Purchase Price of $255,000. After one month, the home was still on the market. We resubmitted our offer of $255,000 and the bank stayed firm at their slightly lowered Asking Price of $284,000. We decided not to budge and continued to wait out this opportunity. After two months, Mr. Swanson, the REO bank manager, lowered the Asking Price to $279,000. Again, we resubmitted our offer of $255,000 and the seller countered with $277,000. We stayed firm and returned to our strategy of waiting it out.

At the end of three months, we called Ms. Bernard who advised us that Mr. Swanson decided not to renew the listing with her and was signing another REO agent in town. We checked in with Mr. Swanson and he told us the listing was going to Cheryl Aberbach. We had made offers on many of her REO properties but hadn't yet made a purchase through her. With Ms. Aberbach, the house at 34 Sebastien Street was listed at $275,000.

We knew this property had already sat for more than three months and we knew the agent hadn't yet exerted much time or cost marketing it. We put forward an idea for a win-win solution. When we contacted Ms. Aberbach, we explained that we already knew the property so she wouldn't even have to let us in to preview it. We asked if she'd be willing to receive a reduced commission, considering she wouldn't have to do much work if we put a contract on 34 Sebastien Street within 48 hours. We pointed out that this deal would forgo splitting the commissions with a buyer's agent and she would receive the full commission. (In many residential markets, the real estate sales commission is split, with half going to the buyer's real estate agent, if a buyer is represented by an agent, and half to the seller's agent.) She would get it all.

As we had hoped, she offered to accept a reduced commission of $5,000 (she agreed to this because this deal represented very little work for her). This was less than half of the commission she would have received if the property had sold for $275,000 and she had split the commission with a buyer's agent (assuming the price wasn't further reduced). However, she had done very little work.

The main point of this example is that we didn't budge from our Maximum Purchase Price. Instead, we used the change in REO agents to leverage the bank's real estate commissions while waiting for the peak sales season to end. For us, this purchase transaction was an exercise in patience and creativity.

We hoped ABC Bank would appreciate this opportunity. After all, we knew the bank would probably continue to have a hard time selling the property because September had rolled around. With kids back in school, many families simply won't be moving any time soon. They were currently asking $275,000. However, they would have cleared only $258,500 after paying a full 6 percent in real estate commissions (assuming a buyer paid the full Asking Price). With our offer, the bank would clear $250,000 (our Maximum Purchase Price offer of $255,000 minus the agent's $5,000 commission).

We were now only $8,500 apart. We weren't sure what the bank would do. However, we were a lot closer than we were before.

Mr. Swanson and the bank knew we weren't budging and recognized the opportunity to move this house off the bank's books without further delay. We bought it for $255,000 within one week of Ms. Aberbach's listing agreement.

In the end, 34 Sebastien Street turned into a great investment for us. Just as important, we maintained our credibility with two key REO agents. We maintained a professional and respectful relationship with Ms. Bernard, plus she knew that our last offer would always mean our best offer. We built credibility with Ms. Aberbach, who appreciated our professionalism and creativity. Finally, we added to our credibility with a key REO bank manager, Mr. Swanson, who learned that we were always professional and respectful, plus he witnessed our "stick-to-itiveness" as we kept with the property and our Maximum Purchase Price throughout the sales life cycle.

A final thought on credibility: Be careful when you ask an agent to reduce his or her commission. Because it's often the agent's sole source of income, we reserve this request for special situations. After all, you don't want to negatively impair all that valuable credibility and goodwill you hope to build with a key REO agent over a few thousand dollars.

5

GOLDEN KEY 4—CALCULATE MAXIMUM PURCHASE PRICES

The Maximum Purchase Price is the most you should pay for a property for it to be a good investment. It is the top price after any and all negotiations have been completed, and it's often referred to as the *ceiling price*. The Maximum Purchase Price factors in all costs, plus your Total Investor Discount. Your ability to determine this amount each time you find a good property to buy—and your self-control not to pay more each time you negotiate—should ultimately play a big role in your success to consistently Buy Even Lower.

Determining the Maximum Purchase Price and exercising self-control may seem like simple tasks. But if you've ever purchased real estate, you know how hard it can be to determine exactly what to pay for a property and how easily you can get caught up in the heat of the negotiations. In this chapter, we'll show you how to calculate the Maximum Purchase Price. In the next two chapters (Golden Keys 5 and 6), we'll show you strategies to help negotiate purchases of properties without exceeding your Maximum Purchase Price.

MAXIMUM PURCHASE PRICE DEPENDS ON YOUR INVESTMENT STRATEGY

For Golden Key 1, you learned that different investment strategies carry different short-term and long-term profits, risks, and required Minimum Investor Discounts when you buy a property.

As a brief refresher, the Buy and Flip investment strategy relies on big, fast profits. You buy the property and sell it for a profit as quickly as possible. However, because a slow-to-sell property can quickly eat into your profits, this strategy's associated risk often requires a Minimum Investor Discount Percentage of 20 to 30 percent or more.

The Buy and Hold investment strategy is built around achieving profits slowly over a long period of time. You purchase the property, usually rent it, and eventually profit from the appreciation when the property is sold. Because you have a long time horizon in which to make your profits, this strategy has little risk and you can look for a much smaller Minimum Investor Discount Percentage (often 5 to 10 percent) than with other strategies when purchasing properties.

The Buy and Lease/Purchase investment strategy is a hybrid of the other two strategies. Sometimes the lease/purchasers exercise their option to purchase quickly after you have purchased the property. Other times, it may take a few years for the lease/purchasers to exercise their option. In some instances, they simply may not exercise their option to purchase the property and you will re-lease/purchase it. Therefore, this strategy yields a combination of big profits in the short term and intermediate term and slow profits over the long term, placing the risks with this strategy in the middle of the other two strategies. Often, a Minimum Investor Discount Percentage of 10 to 20 percent should be used when buying properties with this strategy.

When buying properties, you may come up against another type of buyer: the retail buyer. These are purchasers who intend to live in or use the property themselves. These include families looking to buy a single-family house, empty nesters looking for a smaller home because their kids have moved out, business professionals who are relocating their offices, and so on. Regardless of who they are or why they are looking, many retail buyers won't hesitate to buy the property without a discount. After all, they expect to profit by avoiding future rent payments and recognizing appreciation on the property over the long term, plus they gain additional value from the use and enjoyment of the property while they own it.

As discussed for Golden Key 1, when you select your investment strategy, be sure to determine your Maximum Investor Discount Percentage every time you buy a property. Don't be surprised if you come up against retail buyers and other investors who do not think the same way. Some of these investors simply pick a number that feels right. Others follow along in the negotiation process without a plan, stopping when they either acquire the property or reach a point at which they "feel" that the property is no longer a good buy. These investment strategies (or lack thereof) are extremely risky. This lack of structure often leads to losses, not profits.

Be sure to follow a clearly defined structure when analyzing properties and always determine the maximum amount you will pay for an investment property before beginning the negotiation process. This improves your chance of not overpaying for a property. Even with our years of experience, we sometimes find it difficult not to become caught up in the excitement and energy of the negotiation process. Preestablishing the Maximum Purchase Price helps control these urges.

The bottom line is that people buy properties for a variety of reasons and in a multitude of ways. Select your investment strategy, determine your Minimum Investor Discount Percentage, and calculate your Maximum Purchase Price. Once you've done all this, let your Maximum Purchase Price guide you to the properties you should profitably buy and don't become frustrated if another investor or retail buyer pays more than your strategy allows.

MAXIMUM PURCHASE PRICE FORMULA

Again, the Maximum Purchase Price is the most you should pay for an investment property after factoring in your Total Investor Discount, Repair and Improvement Costs, and Other Costs. The Maximum Purchase Price formula includes the following four variables (see Figure 5.1):

1. Fair Market Value (FMV): The value of the property in a condition that's comparable to similar nearby properties

2. Repair and Improvement Costs (R&I): The costs to repair and improve the property so it's in the condition of comparable properties

3. Other Costs (OC): The miscellaneous costs such as legal, financing, utilities, and advertising required while you fix up and market the property

4. Total Investor Discount (TID): The total discount an investor needs to make a reasonable profit on the property based on the investor's chosen investment strategy and other factors

The Maximum Purchase Price is the Fair Market Value minus the Repair and Improvement Costs, Other Costs, and Total Investor Discount.

Some investors believe that to arrive at the Maximum Purchase Price, you should determine the Fair Market Value of the property in its current condition and add the Repair and Improvement

Figure 5.1 *Maximum Purchase Price*

$$MPP = FMV - R\&I - OC - TID$$

Use this equation to arrive at your Maximum Purchase Price when purchasing a property: Your Maximum Purchase Price (MPP) equals the Fair Market Value (FMV) minus the Repair and Improvement Costs (R&I), Other Costs (OC), and Total Investor Discount (TID).

Costs before subtracting the Other Costs and Total Investor Discount. However, following this methodology is more difficult and cuts into your profits.

First, it's easier to determine the value of any asset when you can compare it to the value of similar assets. Therefore, by assuming the property will be in the same condition as many other similar surrounding properties, you can start your analysis by using the average Fair Market Value of other properties nearby and in good condition. Next, you can modify the Fair Market Value for your specific property by subtracting or adding to the average Fair Market Value of the other properties based on particulars that are missing or extra features your target property offers that the average properties do not possess.

On the other hand, if you try to determine the Fair Market Value of your property based on its current condition, it will be difficult (sometimes considerably difficult) to find any comparable properties. In other words, if your target property needs substantial repair work, it will probably be difficult for you to find other nearby properties (sometimes even a single property) in similar condition. Therefore, determining the Fair Market Value of the property in its current condition is much more about guesswork, which you want to avoid as much as possible to consistently Buy Even Lower and be a successful real estate investor.

Second, if you choose to start with the Fair Market Value in the property's current condition, then you're also likely to move further off course once you add in the Repair and Improvement Costs. Why? Because the costs for repairs and improvements rarely equate exactly to the value they add to the property. For example, painting the outside of a property may cost $5,000. However, this fresh, new paint job may add $10,000 to the value of the property to transform it from "ugly and awful" to beautiful. Or the new paint job may only add $2,000 to the property's value if the old paint was just a bit weathered. Also, adding a bathroom to a house to make it comparable to surrounding houses may cost $10,000. However, this may add $20,000 in value. We hope you see how our formula helps ensure you don't shortchange your profits when making repairs and improvements.

If you're planning to buy undeveloped property and develop it, you probably won't want to use this formula. Most land developers use a much more complex formula to assess their purchases. We suggest you learn more about buying and developing properties from those who specialize in this area.

One final point: The Maximum Purchase Price formula is not a perfect be-all and end-all; it relies on rules of thumb (inexact guidelines). It requires the investor to make subjective assumptions—in some instances, educated guesses. In other words, the Maximum Purchase Price is simply a tool to give you a reasonable idea of what you should pay for a property as an investor—it is not an exact science. Therefore, we encourage novice investors to be conservative and err by determining a Maximum Purchase Price that is too low as opposed to too high. After all, it's always better not to buy a property than to pay too much for it.

FAIR MARKET VALUE

The Fair Market Value is the value of a property in a condition that's comparable to the nearby properties it competes against in the retail market. If the property is a house, condominium, apartment building, or office building, then the Fair Market Value is the value of the property after the investor makes all appropriate repairs and improvements for this property comparable to similar surrounding properties.

The best way to determine the Fair Market Value is with *comps,* which is short for *comparables.* Comps are data sheets describing properties that are for sale and have already sold in the area. They are usually inexpensive or free. You can obtain them from:

- Local real estate agents
- Internet services (such as Realtor.com, Propsmart.com, and Oodle.com)

- Local newspaper Web sites
- Local government offices

Local real estate agents often have access to the best comps. The reason for this is that they usually must join a local real estate agent (Realtor) association, and one of the benefits is access to the local database of properties sold and for sale. Two of the most prominent databases in many places are the multiple listing service (MLS) and first multiple listing service (FMLS). If you're working with an agent to find properties, then you should have access to this data. If not, you may want to consider paying an agent for the data, becoming an agent and joining the association for this benefit, or simply joining as an associate member (which we've heard is available in some places). This comp data is usually up-to-date. The only downside is that it may include only properties sold or for sale by a real estate agent, not properties sold or for sale directly by owner (without an agent).

As for Internet services and local newspaper Web sites, currently these sources of data are not as helpful as one might expect. Yes, there are now many Web sites out there with real estate data, such as *zillow.com, realestateabc.com, propertyshark.com, realtor.com, yahoo.com, homegain.com, domania.com,* and the Web site of your local newspaper. However, most of these Web sites specialize in certain geographic areas and most of this real estate data is for properties currently on the market "for sale." Very little of it, in most instances, is "past sales" data. Also, much of the past sales data may not be as comprehensive as what is available from your real estate agent database. Since you're looking for recent past sales data (as well as current properties for sale) these sites often don't give you all the comp data you need. We expect this to improve over time.

Local government offices, such as the tax office in many counties, may be your best source of recent past sales comp data. After all, every sale in a community is usually recorded by the local government and available to the public. In fact, most past sales data are obtained by other data services from these offices. However, physically going to these offices every time you need data and manually searching through books (as is often required) or even their computer system can be rather cumbersome and time-consuming. We've heard that some government offices are now putting their data on the Internet. Therefore, due to the value of the data and time savings, it may be worth checking into this in your local community.

> **B**eware: **L**ocal **T**ax **A**ppraisers, **B**ad **D**ata
>
> In many communities, tax appraisal data is available to the public. Many inexperienced investors would expect local tax appraisers to be very skilled in the area of determining the Fair Market Value of a property. Unfortunately, based on our experience and what we've heard from many others, tax appraisals are often much lower than the actual Fair Market Value of the property. One reason is that in some communities, the appraisals don't get updated on a regular basis. Another reason may be that it's the best way for the appraiser to avoid appeals from angry property owners, which can be time-consuming. Additionally, most tax appraisers never actually enter the property, but rely on data such as total square footage, number of bedrooms and bathrooms, and so on that they believe to be accurate (but often aren't) to do their analysis. Whatever the reason, be careful if you choose to rely on tax appraisals for your comps.

When analyzing comps, compare the values of properties that are, indeed, comparable. Avoid comparing apples to oranges. That means if you're analyzing a three-bedroom house that doesn't have a finished basement and a similar three-bedroom house does have one, then they aren't perfectly comparable. You'll have to adjust your analysis to make it an apple-to-apple comparison. Often you can adjust prices by comparing several comps. For example, comparing two comps with finished basements and two without can reveal a consistent $15,000 difference. Therefore, finished basements in that neighborhood add approximately $15,000 in value to comparable properties without finished basements.

Also, search for comps within the same neighborhood or within a radius of a few miles. If there aren't enough, you may choose to expand to the broader community or even outside the community. Remember, the farther away you move from your target property, the more risk you will be taking that you'll be comparing an apple to an orange.

As you perform apples-to-apples comparisons, you'll better determine the accurate Fair Market Value of your target property. Read comps to identify increases or decreases in prices of properties. Get a feel for the overall values, plus any tendency for values to be inching up, inching down, or remaining stable. Try to only review comps that are fewer than 12 months old to obtain the most current information possible. If few comps exist, go back as far as 18 months. However, four or five comps from within 12 months are usually more valuable than 10 or 15 comps that are more than a year old.

To glean more information, you can gather various viewpoints by checking with multiple real estate agents. They often have knowledge and insights regarding neighborhoods in which they list properties. You can sometimes find local agents' names on the comps or you can obtain names from For Sale signs in your target community. Local agents are frequently biased and will often praise the neighborhood highly because they're trying to sell properties in it. For the real scoop, consider telling agents you are an investor, *not* a prospect for their listings. These agents may not want to spend as much time speaking with you. However, they may provide you with better, more valuable information.

As mentioned for Golden Key 3, regardless of what the comps and local real estate agents say, get a good feel for the neighborhood, community, and geographic area by driving or walking around. See if the other properties in the community are well kept. If numerous properties in the area need paint, new roofs, or yard work, this can suggest a potential problem on the horizon. If you can't find properties in obvious need of care and attention, this is a good sign, indicating a stable community with properties that should retain their value and eventually see increases.

For residential property, drive the neighborhood and pull For Sale flyers to gather information. Also take time to walk into "open houses," which are usually held on weekends, as part of your research. Homes with open houses tend to cater to retail buyers and typically don't sell at a discount. But by visiting open houses, you'll get a feel for how people fix them up and which attributes stand out. Knowing this helps you immeasurably when deciding which, if any, improvements you'd need to make to your target property. Also, search the Internet and read local newspapers for more information on the community.

When assessing the community, look for special characteristics, trends, and new developments. Try to determine whether highways, parks, retail stores, and schools are scheduled to be constructed. If possible, assess how they'll impact the community and its future property values. You may want to talk to people in the area and learn what they're saying about the plans.

> **Watch for Neighborhoods That Will "Catch Fire"**
>
> Particular neighborhoods in a community can "catch fire" or become the trendy place to live. We purchased a property in an area of Atlanta that was poised for significant appreciation. New shops were opening up, people were moving in, and a new highway extension was being completed on the outskirts of this community. Recognizing this, we factored it into our Fair Market Value. Comps alone didn't give us all the information we needed to ascertain the accurate Fair Market Value because they didn't reflect the future interest this community might generate.

Here's the bottom line with Fair Market Values for properties: In many instances, you won't find an exact match for your property. Often you'll find similar properties with a few different characteristics or similar properties that were sold more than 12 months ago. Nevertheless, if you follow our suggestions, you should come up with a usable range within which the Fair Market

Value for your property should fall. Once you do, then be conservative and work with a value at the low end of the range.

REPAIR AND IMPROVEMENT COSTS

Every property we've ever bought has had some Repair and Improvement Costs that needed to be factored in to determine a Maximum Purchase Price. Therefore, unless you're going to buy undeveloped land and keep it that way for the long haul, Repair and Improvement Costs will probably play an important role in helping you Buy Even Lower.

Most of the properties we've purchased have needed significant repairs and improvements because, as investors, we're looking for properties to buy at a discount. Many of the best-priced deals need work. Not surprisingly, properties that don't need work get sold to a retail buyer (someone who will live in the house or use the building for his or her office) at or close to the Fair Market Value.

The following paragraphs detail our definitions of repair costs and improvement costs. Remember, your goal is to make your property *comparable* to surrounding properties, not better than them.

Repair Costs

These include any costs needed to put the property in good livable or usable condition. Repairs needed to meet this criterion include anything that a buyer, renter, or lease/purchaser would find functionally wrong with the property when you put it on the market.

For example, you'll need to fix or replace anything that doesn't operate properly: a leaky roof, broken window, bad furnace, inoperable air conditioner, and weak plumbing pressure. Overly worn or stained carpet, painted or wallpapered walls with

Beware: Real Estate Appraisers

Some new investors presume getting an appraisal is the best way to determine the Fair Market Value of the property they are purchasing. In fact, property owners sometimes get a real estate appraisal before they sell a property. After all, an appraiser is an expert who should be able to give you an exact number for the value of the house. But hiring an appraiser every time you consider buying a property can be expensive. Appraisers often charge from $250 to $500 and more, depending on the size of the property and other particulars. This adds up to a lot of money over time. Additionally, even though they're supposed to be experts, most appraisers won't be as thorough as you will. They often have many appraisals to complete and will only spend a few hours working on the property in which you're interested. Unless it's an expensive property, most investors don't use an appraisal to determine its Fair Market Value. However, if you're just starting out, you may want to consider this option.

While most investors don't get an appraisal for each offer they make, they sometimes rely on appraisals to double-check their numbers. Specifically, if the seller accepts your purchase offer, your lender will usually require that you hire an appraiser to conduct an appraisal before it gives you a loan for the property. The lender wants an experienced, unbiased party to confirm its investment will be safe. In other words, because most lenders secure their loans with property, the lender must ensure each property is worth more than the loan value in case the investor defaults. If the appraisal comes in too low, the lender probably won't give you the loan. You can then walk away from the property (as long as you have the proper provision in your contract, which will be discussed for Golden Key 5) or question the appraiser on his or her conclusions. Interestingly, almost all of the appraisals we've received have come in right at or close to the sales price we have negotiated with the seller (this is particularly interesting when you consider that all of our offers include a Total Investor Discount). This is probably because appraisers only spend a few hours on each appraisal and don't want to cause more work for themselves (a much higher or lower appraisal would result in questions from us and the lender).

smudges, and cracked tiles or torn linoleum floors are also examples of functional problems you'll need to address. Be sure to factor in new door locks because most people find it a functional problem when the former inhabitant has keys, and thus access, to the property. Whether you fix or replace each of these items, you would classify all labor and material costs associated with taking care of these items as repair costs.

When considering repair costs, remember that your goal is to get the property in *good* condition, not *perfect* condition. Some rooms may need painting and wallpapering, while others don't. Just because the carpet has a few minor holes and spots, it doesn't mean that the entire property needs new carpet. Consider replacing the most worn sections and professionally steam cleaning the rest. On the other hand, if spots still show or the carpet has too many holes to touch up, the property may need new carpet after all. Again, be careful when determining your repair costs.

Here's a challenging example: Just because an air conditioner looks old and has a problem, that doesn't mean you have to replace it if it can be repaired. On the other hand, if it looks old, you may need to replace it simply because a potential buyer may believe it will quit working in the near future.

If you're experienced and can do the repairs, this may be enough to accurately assess the property's needed repairs and associated costs. However, if you aren't experienced or can't assess these types of problems, then you may choose to lean on those who can. Some would suggest hiring an inspector to assess the property. Chances are he or she also can recommend people or companies to fix any problems. They may also find problems that you've overlooked. It can become very expensive to hire an inspector for every property on which you consider making an offer. Inspectors often charge $250 to $500 or more. For this reason, we have a provision in our contract that allows us to perform a thorough inspection after both parties agree to the contract terms and protects us from problems we may have overlooked. (This is covered in detail for Golden Key 5.) Accordingly, we don't hire inspectors to help us assess a property when we're determining the Maximum Purchase Price. We simply try to spot as many problems as possible and often rely on companies and contractors to give us the costs to take care of those problems. (Try to use companies that don't charge to provide estimates.)

Be careful with companies and contractors who assess the problems and perform the work, too. Many companies would prefer selling you something new rather than fixing something old. Be sure to ask for the costs to fix or replace the item. You may want to have two experienced people or companies look at the items on your repair list to obtain a second opinion, especially for expensive ones. For example, we once viewed a property with a potentially costly mold problem. One company advised us it would cost $40,000 to address the mold issues. We asked a second company that did mold assessments only and didn't perform treatments to assess the property. They determined the issue was minor and recommended a different company to handle the problem. This option cost substantially less money than the original estimate.

Getting a referral from someone you trust (a friend, fellow investor, real estate attorney, etc.) is usually the best way to find a good company or contractor. You can also find those people in the *Yellow Pages,* the newspaper, or on the Internet. Check out the businesses' and contractors' reputations with your local Better Business Bureau. Always ask for references—and check them.

Improvement Costs

These include any costs necessary to get the property in the condition comparable to nearby properties. *Necessary* improvements are any *features* a buyer, renter, or lease/purchaser would find clearly "missing" from the property when you put it on the market.

For example, if most of the houses in the neighborhood have updated kitchens and the house you're looking at has old appliances, countertops, cabinets, and wallpaper, then your target property may be "missing" an updated kitchen. The same holds true for other rooms in a residential property, especially bathrooms. A bathroom with shag carpet and green wallpaper from the 1970s, even in good condition, may need to be upgraded.

Sometimes the necessary improvement is the number of bedrooms and bathrooms or the size of the garage. All the homes in the neighborhood may have fenced backyards and yours doesn't have a fence. All comparable homes may have security systems but yours doesn't have one. Maybe your property is "missing" a swimming pool.

If most of the comparable properties have three bedrooms and yours only has two, consider converting another room into a bedroom or adding onto the structure to create one. All the labor and materials costs associated with this project make up your improvement costs for this property.

If this is a commercial property, consider the comparable sizes of offices, storefronts, and so on. Perhaps you need to factor in whether there are enough bathrooms and a security system. All the costs to make these changes and additions are improvement costs.

When considering improvement costs, be careful. It's easy to compare your target property to others and think about how much more valuable your property would be if it had certain additional features. While most of these missing features would add value to the property, sometimes the cost of adding them is more than the actual value they would add. Once you've compiled your list of potential improvements, be sure to factor in only those you deem necessary to get the property in a condition comparable to those surrounding it.

Remember, your goal is to make this property work for you as an investment you can buy at a discount now and earn profit on in the future. You walk a fine line with improvement costs because a significant amount of costs factored into the property will appreciably lower your Maximum Purchase Price. Therefore, it may be difficult for you to make the sellers understand why you're offering such a substantially discounted amount off the price they are trying to sell the property for. Also, the more improvements you undertake to a property, the more risk you have of eating into your profits due to unforeseen cost overruns, time delays, and other headaches to prepare the property to sell, rent, or lease/purchase.

Don't forget that your goal is to upgrade your property so it's *comparable* to surrounding properties, not better than them. In fact, most real estate experts agree that it's better to have the least-improved property in the community than the most-improved property because communities tend to pull up the values of properties at the bottom and pull down those at the top. Therefore, if all other houses in the neighborhood have a swimming pool, you may choose to put in a pool. But if only *some* have pools, then your decision should be easy—don't take this unnecessary risk. In fact, by choosing *not* to add a pool, you can ride the coattails of property values of the neighborhood houses that do have pools. If you do add a pool and take these types of risks regularly, then you'll have a harder time consistently growing your profits over the long run.

How can you assess whether an improvement is necessary? You can look at comps to assess the basics such as square footage, bedrooms, bathrooms, garages, and so on. You can view other comparable properties that are for sale, rent, or lease/purchase. You can also ask local real estate agents who specialize in your type of property.

To accurately assess improvement costs, ask experienced companies or contractors for estimates to perform the work. Referrals from people you trust are the best way to find these companies and contractors. Ask for and check references. Again, your local Better Business Bureau may have helpful information on these companies and people. Because improvements are usually big-ticket items, be sure to obtain at least two estimates.

One final point: For both repair costs and improvement costs, be sure to always include a buffer. Rarely do these costs come in exactly on budget—usually they come in over budget. Therefore, you may want to add 5 to 10 percent (or more) to the estimates as your buffer.

OTHER COSTS

Other Costs are costs necessary to purchase the property and get it sold, rented, or lease/purchased. These costs are the hidden enemy of profits. Some investors believe Other Costs are negligible and don't factor them into the cost of buying their properties. In reality, Other Costs often end up taking a big bite out of an investor's profits. Individual expenses may be relatively small but, taken together, these costs can add up to several thousands of dollars and sometimes even tens of thousands of dollars.

Other Costs include (see Figure 5.2)

- Legal Costs (LEG),
- Finance Costs (FIN),
- Taxes and Insurance Costs (T&I),
- Mortgage Payment Costs (MORT),
- Utility Costs (UC),
- Marketing Costs (MARK),
- Real Estate Agent Costs (REA), and
- Miscellaneous Costs (MISC).

The following paragraphs briefly describe each of the components of Other Costs.

Legal Costs. These are the legal fees you pay for work performed by your real estate attorney for the property purchase. Sometimes, you can control these costs by choosing the closing

Figure 5.2 *Other Costs*

> OC = LEG + FIN + T&I + MORT + UC + MARK + REA + MISC
>
> To determine your total Other Costs (OC), add all the costs for Legal (LEG), Finance (FIN), Taxes and Insurance (T&I), Utility (UC), Mortgage Payment (MORT), Marketing (MARK), Real Estate Agent (REA), and Miscellaneous (MISC) Costs.

attorney. Other times, the lender will require you to use a particular attorney. In the contract, the seller may agree to pay all or part of this item. However, until you can negotiate this cost down or away, you need to factor the entire amount into your Other Costs.

Legal Costs can be as low as a few hundred dollars or as high as thousands of dollars. These costs vary from state to state. To learn about potential legal costs in your area, ask local real estate attorneys, real estate agents, and the lender you are considering using. Legal Costs can sometimes be financed into your loan, so also check with your lender about this.

Finance Costs. These include the fees the financial institution requires you to pay to receive a loan. These costs include origination fees, processing fees, appraisal fees, and more. Fees vary depending on the type of loan, the amount of down payment, and the term of the loan. Find out if your lender will let you finance some or all of the Finance Costs into your loan. These fees may vary significantly from lender to lender, so talk with several lenders before choosing one. Become familiar with the lenders' different Finance Costs.

Finance Costs also include the cost of money if you're using a line of credit to finance your purchase. These costs will usually be low, but be sure to include this expense if you use the Buy and Flip or Buy and Lease/Purchase strategy.

As with Legal Costs, you may be able to negotiate with the seller to pay all or some of the Finance Costs. However, until the seller agrees to pay them, don't forget to include the Finance Costs in your Other Costs calculation.

Taxes and Insurance Costs. This is the amount of taxes and insurance you will pay from the time you buy the property until the time you sell, rent, or lease/purchase it. For this calculation (determining your Maximum Purchase Price), Taxes and Insurance Costs don't include the entire annual amount that you'll owe on this property.

Taxes owed on the property in previous years are public record; you can usually obtain these from the local tax office, online tax records, or even comps. If you're buying a house, make sure you remember that, as an investor, you won't be receiving a homestead exemption like the previous owners did if they lived in the home.

Your insurance agent can give you a firm insurance estimate. Be prepared for the insurance premium to be higher than you're used to paying for a homeowner's insurance policy, though it should not be significantly higher.

Unless you're using the Buy and Flip investment strategy, Taxes and Insurance Costs will be an ongoing obligation. Therefore, if you plan to rent or lease/purchase your properties, factor these costs into your anticipated annual costs and monthly cash flow. If you're buying undeveloped land, these costs may have a huge impact on your purchase because you probably won't have any (or much) incoming revenue streams to offset them.

Mortgage Payment Costs. These costs are the monthly principal and interest payments you'll make to your lender. Similar to Taxes and Insurance Costs, you'll need to estimate the amount of your Mortgage Payment Costs for the property before reselling, renting, or lease/purchasing it. Your lender can give you this information. Also, there are calculators and Web sites that will calculate this for you when you input the amount of the loan, its interest rate, and its duration. As with Taxes and Insurance Costs, make a point of understanding how this will affect your annual costs and monthly cash flow if you plan to rent, lease/purchase, or hold undeveloped land for appreciation.

Note that mortgage payments are usually made one month in arrears. This means you don't have to make a payment the first month you own the property. Check with your lender on this point.

Utility Costs. This includes all costs for electricity, gas, water, and any other utility to the property before you resell, rent, or lease/purchase it. You can contact the local utility companies for estimates. Sometimes they require deposits or start-up fees. For most undeveloped land, you should be able to ignore this cost.

Marketing Costs. If you choose to market your properties directly without using a real estate agent (as we usually do), then you need to include the costs for this activity in your Marketing Costs. These costs typically include advertising, signs, and flyers. You can call the newspaper to obtain advertising costs (or check its Web site), find costs for signs at your local home improvement store, and ask for flyer costs from your local printer or print flyers on your own computer. (We have a professionally designed sign that we use repeatedly with our various purchases. We personalize the sign for each property by indicating the number of bedrooms and bathrooms.)

Real Estate Agent Costs. You may incur these costs during the initial purchase of the property and also during the flip, rent, and lease/purchase phase. These costs can be significant; be careful because they can eat up chunks of profit. Fortunately, most sellers are willing to pay Real Estate Agent Costs when you purchase the property. However, confirm this when you're considering a property that has one or more real estate agents involved.

Because Real Estate Agent Costs can be significant when you sell, rent, or lease/purchase a property (often 6 to 7 percent of the selling price), we avoid using a real estate agent whenever possible. If you use one, factor the estimated fees associated with these activities into the Other Costs category.

Modified real estate agent opportunities are available to investors today. These allow you to access local listing services that agents use without paying full real estate commissions. One of the most common services is the multiple listing service (MLS). In some communities, it costs as little as $500 to post a property on the listing services; you take the responsibilities normally handled by the selling agent. However, you must still pay the full buyer's agent commission to any buyers who purchase using buyer's agents. Therefore, the seller may pay half of the standard Real Estate Agent Costs (3 to 3½ versus 6 to 7 percent).

Miscellaneous Costs. These include unplanned costs. Even the experienced investor can't always make everything go according to plan, so factor in Miscellaneous Costs as a buffer. You may choose to use a flat amount such as $1,000, $5,000, or $10,000, depending on the Fair Market Value of the property, the number of repairs and improvements, or other factors. You may also choose to apply a percentage of the Fair Market Value, such as 1, 2, 5, or 10 percent, depending on the same factors.

We vary between flat amounts and percentages. We usually build in a buffer of at least a few thousand dollars for properties with small repair and improvement projects (e.g., for a property with a Fair Market Value of $200,000 and minimal repairs and improvements costs, we might choose 2 to 3 percent or $2,000 to $3,000 for miscellaneous costs). For properties needing significant repair and improvement, we often add a buffer of $10,000 or more (e.g., if the same $200,000 property had $50,000 of repairs and improvements costs, then we might choose 5 to 10 percent or $5,000 to $10,000 for Miscellaneous Costs).

TOTAL INVESTOR DISCOUNT

The Total Investor Discount is the total discount an investor needs to make a reasonable profit on the property. The TID is determined by using a Total Investor Discount Percentage (TID%) and multiplying it by the Fair Market Value of the property (see Figure 5.3).

Figure 5.3 *Total Investor Discount*

$$TID = TID\% \times FMV$$

To arrive at the dollar amount for your Total Investor Discount (TID), select the Total Investor Discount Percentage (TID%) and multiply it by the property's Fair Market Value (FMV).

How do you arrive at the specific Total Investor Discount Percentage? The Total Investor Discount Percentage comprises the following four variables (see Figure 5.4):

1. Minimum Investor Discount Percentage (MID%): The smallest amount of profit you should receive to buy the property based on your investment strategy
2. Repair and Improvement Hassle Percentage (RIH%): The additional discount you should receive to deal with repairing and improving the property
3. Negative Property Attributes Percentage (NPA%): The additional discount you should receive due to a problem with the property that's too expensive or complex to change
4. Length of Time on the Market Percentage (LTM%): The additional discount you should receive due to a property sitting on the market for an extended period of time

As with the other components of the Maximum Purchase Price formula, you will use a number of assumptions and rules of thumb to determine the Total Investor Discount Percentage. Additionally, this may be the most subjective component of the formula. Accordingly, we advise novice investors to be especially conservative when determining the Total Investor Discount Percentage to ensure they obtain their anticipated Buy Even Lower profits. The following paragraphs describe each component of the Total Investor Discount Percentage.

Figure 5.4 *Total Investor Discount Percentage*

TID% = MID% + RIH% + NPA% + LTM%

To determine the Total Investor Discount Percentage (TID%) for a property, add the Minimum Total Investor Discount Percentage (MID%), the Repair and Improvement Hassle Percentage (RIH%), the Negative Property Attribute Percentage (NPA%), and the Length of Time on the Market Percentage (LTM%).

Minimum Investor Discount Percentage. This is usually the easiest variable of the formula to find because you should have decided on it, or at least thought about it, when you went through Golden Key 1—Determine your Minimum Investor Discount. If you have any questions on the appropriate MID% to use, please refer back to Golden Key 1.

Repair and Improvement Hassle Percentage. This is the amount of extra Total Investor Discount you should receive for the time and effort you put into the property to repair and improve it (we call it the *hassle factor*). Whether you do the work yourself or have someone else do it, you should get compensated for dealing with the hassle. The bigger the problem, the bigger the Repair and Improvement Hassle Percentage.

Most buyers who will live in or use the property and many investors simply don't want to deal with problems. That's why realistic sellers of these types of properties are often willing to accept this additional discount.

Not all properties need repairs or improvements; many are in mint condition. However, as we've discussed, most of these will be sold to retail buyers (people who will live in or use the property) because they're willing to buy the property at or close to the Fair Market Value. These properties often don't need to be discounted because most investors won't be buying these types of properties. If you do, the RIH% will be zero.

For properties needing repairs and improvements, the rule of thumb we often use for the RIH% is *1 percent for every 3 percent*—that is, you want 1 percent additional Total Investor Discount for every 3 percent of repairs and improvements based on the Fair Market Value of the property.

For example, if a house with a Fair Market Value of $100,000 needs $3,000 worth of repairs and improvements, then you'd use a 1 percent Repair and Improvement Hassle Percentage because the $3,000 is 3 percent of the Fair Market Value of the property. On the other hand, if an office building has a Fair Market Value of $500,000 and needs $30,000 worth of repairs and improvements, you'd ask for a 2 percent RIH%. The $30,000 is 6 percent of the Fair Market Value and the "1 percent for every 3 percent" rule of thumb equals 2 percent for the RIH%.

Important note: For properties needing little of your time and effort to repair and improve, you may choose to decrease the total RIH%; for properties needing an excessive amount, you may choose to increase it. For example, a house simply needing some paint may require little of your time and effort (simply hire a painter and select paint colors). On the other hand, if the same house needed an updated kitchen or bathroom or new support beams, these projects may require more of your time and effort (even if the actual cost to make the repairs and improvements is the same as the easier paint project). In the first case, you may choose to reduce the RIH% by 0.5 to 1 percent and, in the second case, increase it by 0.5 to 1 percent or more. Like the rest of this formula, the RIH% is subjective and you will get better at determining it with experience. Therefore, for novice investors, we encourage you to often stick to the rule of thumb—1 percent for every 3 percent.

Also, note that when we refer to *time and effort,* we're referring to the time and effort to manage the project, not perform the actual repairs and improvements that a contractor or specialist would perform. If you do perform the actual work, the profits you need to receive for this time and effort should be covered in the Repair and Improvement Costs category (the same profits the contractor or specialist would realize if you paid them).

Negative Property Attributes Percentage. This is the amount of extra discount the investor should receive because of an unappealing feature that can't be reasonably changed due to the cost or complexity of fixing or improving it. Because of this unappealing attribute, the seller will have difficulty selling the property. For example, if a house is on a noticeably smaller lot than others in the neighborhood or is on a busy street, this may be a negative property attribute. Or, a wood exterior and a lot on a big hill may be negative property attributes if all the other houses in the neighborhood have brick exteriors and flat lots.

Don't consider most cosmetic repairs and improvements as negative property attributes; most of those can be reasonably changed. For example, the property may simply need updating from its 1970s look. A property with an unusual layout that can be rectified by knocking down walls or adding on a room may not be a negative property attribute. Depending on the value of the property, these may be reasonably changed and aren't negative property attributes.

What **I**s a **N**egative *Attribute?*

Andy's residence is in a historic section of Atlanta where homes are approximately 100 years old. These houses have been modernized, of course, but the modernization has been restricted by the space limitations of the existing structure. Andy's home had no room for a laundry room on the main level without sacrificing an existing bedroom, which was not an option. The previous homeowner created a laundry room by knocking out a wall and building a small extra room supported by stilts from the bottom level outside the house. Trees alongside the home obstructed the view of this protruding room. It sounds a bit funky but the "outside" laundry room works great. It added a room that most homeowners are looking for in a home in a way that could be "reasonably changed." Consequently, this wouldn't be considered a negative property attribute.

Note: Costs to repair and improve would be included in the Repair and Improvement Costs portion of the Maximum Purchase Price formula. The formula would also include an additional discount in the Repair and Improvement Hassle Percentage to deal with this issue.

For properties with negative property attributes, our rule of thumb for the NPA% is fairly subjective. It can be *as low as 1 to 3 percent* for properties that may not be perceived as a negative property attribute by every potential buyer or renter. On the other end of the spectrum, the NPA% can be *10 percent or more* for larger, more severe problems that potential owners would notice and that would be an issue for most (if not all) prospective buyers or renters. Be careful if you ever consider going above 10 percent. If a property has severely negative attributes, it may be too difficult for you to turn a profit on it—even with the best reselling, renting, or lease/purchase terms.

We once bought a house with approximately 1,200 square feet in a subdivision with houses averaging more than 2,000 square feet. We gave this home an NPA% of 4 percent because we knew it would be difficult to lease/purchase. Fortunately, our lease/purchase terms attracted a good family who eventually purchased the house and we were able to profit appropriately from this purchase.

The **H**ouse *with the* **45-D**egree **S**lope

Remember the ugly and awful house on the 45-degree slope in which the front yard was essentially nonfunctional? It was too steep for kids to play on and the slope was so steep that routine maintenance of the yard would be a challenge. We had to build a retaining wall to address erosion. In fact, the front yard was the primary reason this home had been on the market for four months when we saw it. We knew that once we bought the house, we'd probably have difficulty marketing it. Therefore, we sought a Negative Property Attributes Percentage of 8 percent. Sure enough, when we set appointments with prospective lease/purchasers, we sat in the house and watched as approximately half the people who drove up to the house didn't even get out of their cars. They took one look at the slope of the front yard and drove off. We compensated for this negative attribute by setting the lease payment lower than if the home had a front yard that resembled most of others in the subdivision. We also sweetened the rest of our lease/purchase terms to help maximize the interest of serious candidates. We have lease/purchased this home twice. Each time our marketing period lasted a couple of weeks longer than our average marketing period. However, each time we attracted great lease/purchaser tenants. The second family even purchased the home after their sixth year living there. Again, because we properly factored in the negative property attribute, we were able to profit appropriately from the purchase.

As you can see, the Negative Property Attributes Percentage is the most subjective component of the Maximum Purchase Price formula. There are so many different types of negative attributes and each impacts the Fair Market Value differently. Because this is so subjective, you will need to carefully consider the negative attribute to determine the anticipated impact on reselling, renting, or lease/purchasing the property. The more significant the issue, the greater the percentage discount you'll probably need to secure in order to realize your anticipated profits.

Length of Time on the Market Percentage. This is the extra amount of discount you should be able to receive because the property has been for sale for an extended period of time. Because the property has been on the market for this extended time, the sellers often feel added stress and frustration. Therefore, they're often motivated to sell quickly and willing to give you this additional discount if you ask for it.

For properties that aren't listed with an agent, helpful real estate agents and neighbors can provide this tip about whether a certain property is not selling. When a property is listed with an agent, most listing services show the length of time the property has been on the market, even if the agent has changed.

Is this discount worth pursuing? After all, you may not like taking advantage of other people in stressful situations. We're no different. However, there are some good reasons you should ask for this discount.

First, this property may have earned a bad reputation because it has been on the market for so long. This doesn't happen all the time. However, we have seen firsthand how potential buyers can assume there is a problem with a property simply because it's taking a long time to sell. These people may not be willing to consider purchasing the property for this simple reason.

Second, if the property has been on the market for a long time for the current seller, you may have some related selling, renting, or lease/purchasing challenges. The LTM% helps protect your profits from these situations.

For the Length of Time on the Market Percentage, we usually use a rule of thumb of *1 percent for every month over two months* that a residential property has been on the market. Most residential properties should have a purchase contract on them within a couple of months and most sellers expect this too. The most common listing agreement with a real estate agent for residential property is a three-month listing agreement and many real estate agents feel pressure and stress in the final month before their exclusive listing agreement expires.

For example, if a property has been on the market for six months, the LTM% would be 4 percent (four months of extended period multiplied by 1 percent). A property that has been on the market for a year would have an LTM% of 10 percent. For commercial real estate, you may choose to use 1 percent for every month over three or four because commercial property tends to sell more slowly.

Some investors may use 0.25 percent or 0.5 percent and some may cap this discount at 5 percent. All of these variations can position you for appropriate profits. After all, the length of time on the market may have little relevance to your future profits. The property could have been on the market for a long time primarily due to glaring cosmetic issues, poor marketing, or both. Nonetheless, if a property is on the market for a long time, this can impact the future marketing of the property and many sellers will compensate you for this.

EXAMPLES OF CALCULATING MAXIMUM PURCHASE PRICES

We've covered a lot in this chapter and the formulas can be intimidating to some people. Therefore, before we present some examples, let's do a quick review of the Maximum Purchase Price formula.

Figure 5.5 *Maximum Purchase Price*

$$MPP = FMV - R\&I - OC - TID$$

To determine your Maximum Purchase Price (MPP), start with the property's Fair Market Value (FMV) and subtract Repair and Improvement Costs (R&I), Other Costs (OC), and your Total Investor Discount (TID).

First, as a reminder, the Maximum Purchase Price is the most you should be willing to pay for a property as an investor based on your investment strategy. Assess the property's Fair Market Value, then subtract Repair and Improvement Costs, Other Costs, and your Total Investor Discount. Refer to Figure 5.5 to see the formula for calculating a property's Maximum Purchase Price.

Again, the Fair Market Value is the value of a property in a condition that is comparable to those properties it will compete against in the retail market. Repair and Improvement Costs are the repair costs required to upgrade the property into a good livable or usable condition and improvement costs necessary to upgrade the property into a condition comparable to those nearby to it. Other Costs are the additional expenses necessary from the time of the purchase until the property is sold, rented, or lease/purchased. This category includes Legal, Finance, Taxes and Insurance, Mortgage Payment, Utility, Marketing, Real Estate Agent, and Miscellaneous Costs (see Figure 5.6).

Figure 5.6 *Other Costs*

$$OC = LEG + FIN + T\&I + MORT + UC + MARK + REA + MISC$$

To arrive at your total for Other Costs (OC), combine these expenses: Legal (LEG), Finance (FIN), Taxes and Insurance (T&I), Mortgage Payments (MORT), Utilities (UC), Marketing (MARK), Real Estate Agent (REA), and Miscellaneous (MISC) Costs.

Figure 5.7 *Total Investor Discount*

$$TID = TID\% \times FMV$$

To determine your Total Investor Discount (TID), multiply the Total Investor Discount Percentage (TID%) by the property's Fair Market Value (FMV).

The Total Investor Discount is the cumulative discount you should receive as an investor for buying a particular property. The Total Investor Discount is based on your investment strategy and is the Total Investor Discount Percentage multiplied by the property's Fair Market Value (see Figure 5.7).

The Total Investor Discount Percentage consists of the Minimum Investor Discount Percentage, the Repair and Improvement Hassle Percentage, the Negative Property Attributes Percentage, and the Length of Time on the Market Percentage (see Figure 5.8).

The following examples illustrate how to calculate the Maximum Purchase Price for different properties.

Example 1: The 1970s House in a Ditch

In this example, the comparable houses in this neighborhood in good condition sell for $100,000. This house is a postforeclosure. The bank is currently asking $65,000 for the property. The house needs new paint and carpet throughout. The kitchen and

Figure 5.8 *Total Investor Discount Percentage*

$$TID\% = MID\% + RIH\% + NPA\% + LTM\%$$

To arrive at your Total Investor Discount Percentage (TID%), add your Minimum Investor Discount Percentage (MID%), the Repair and Improvement Hassle Percentage (RIH%), the Negative Property Attributes Percentage (NPA%), and the Length of Time on the Market Percentage (LTM%).

---

bathrooms also need to be updated. This house will need $7,000 in repairs, $8,000 in improvements, and the bank is not making these repairs or improvements. From the outside, the house looks nice, but it sits in what looks like a ditch. The driveway has a steep downward slope, which may explain why it has been on the market for five months. As the investor, you will use the Buy and Lease/Purchase strategy.

You have determined that the Fair Market Value is $100,000 and the Repair and Improvement Costs are $15,000. We'll also assume that Legal Costs are $500, Finance Costs are $2,000, Taxes and Insurance Costs are $500, Mortgage Payment Costs are $1,000, Utility Costs are $500, and Marketing Costs are $500. Additionally, you will not use a real estate agent so you won't need to pay an agent's commission, and Miscellaneous Costs will be $2,500 (a nice buffer, to be on the safe side). Then you add all the expenses in the Other Costs category (see Figure 5.9).

Determining the Total Investor Discount takes some analysis. You are using the Buy and Lease/Purchase strategy, so the Minimum Investor Discount Percentage (MID%) is 10 percent. The Repair and Improvement Costs estimate is $15,000, which equates to 15 percent of the Fair Market Value of $100,000. Therefore, because the rule of thumb we usually use is "1 percent Repair and Improvement Hassle for every 3 percent of Fair Market Value," the Repair and Improvement Hassle Percentage is 5 percent

Figure 5.9 *Calculation of Other Costs*

Legal Costs (LEG)	$500
Finance Costs (FIN)	2,000
Taxes and Insurance Costs (T&I)	500
Mortgage Payment Costs (MORT)	1,000
Utility Costs (UC)	500
Marketing Costs (MARK)	500
Real Estate Agent Costs (REA)	0
Miscellaneous Costs (MISC)	2,500
Other Costs (OC)	$7,500

Figure 5.10 *Calculation of Total Investor Discount Percentage*

TID% = MID% + RIH% + NPA% + LTM%

First, determine the Total Investor Discount Percentage:
TID% = 10% + 5% + 5% + 3%
TID% = 23%

Next, determine the dollar amount of your Total Investor Discount:
TID = TID% × FMV
TID = 23% × $100,000
TID = $23,000

The Total Investor Discount for the house in the ditch is $23,000.

(15 percent divided by 3). See Figure 5.10 for a calculation of Total Investor Discount. Some people may even choose to increase it to 6 percent because of the kitchen and bathroom remodeling project, which may take extra time and effort but, for this example, you'll stick with the 5 percent.

The current cosmetic condition of the property won't impact the marketing of the home once the repairs and improvements are completed, so the only negative property attribute of significance is that the house sits in a ditch. Therefore, you assign 5 percent for the Negative Property Attributes Percentage. For this example, 5 percent may seem like a big discount but many retail buyers or investors will be turned off by a home that has such a steep driveway and may have flooding issues.

Finally, because the home has been on the market for five months, you choose 3 percent for the Length of Time on the Market Percentage—1 percent for every month over two months. At this point, the seller is probably becoming desperate to unload this house.

Now what? We have a Maximum Purchase Price of $54,500 (see Figure 5.11), but the bank is asking $65,000 for this property and its Fair Market Value is $100,000. We've just determined that the maximum you should pay is just over half of the Fair Market Value of the property in fixed-up condition. Why would a bank sell the property to you for this low price?

Figure 5.11 *Calculation of Maximum Purchase Price*

$$MPP = FMV - R\&I - OC - TID$$
$$MPP = \$100,000 - \$15,000 - \$7,500 - \$23,000$$
$$MPP = \$54,500$$

First, let's look at the bank's perspective: This house needs significant work and it sits in a ditch. More important, after five months on the market, this house is tying up the bank's money. Remember, banks are in the business of lending money and every day this house doesn't sell is another day that the bank loses a lending opportunity for this money. Now, the bank may not sell you this property for your Maximum Purchase Price. However, we've had many situations in which financial institutions have sold us properties at approximately 50 percent of the fixed-up Fair Market Value.

On the other hand, if you can get the property at or below your Maximum Purchase Price, this might seem like a great deal on paper. However, unlike a property in mint condition sitting on a flat lot, this property will take some time and effort to fix up and lease/purchase. You also risk cost overruns and additional costs related to delays in preparing the house to market and lease/purchase. Therefore, if you purchase this property at the Maximum Purchase Price, you deserve the significant Total Investor Discount of $23,000. If expenses hold true, this is your profit on this property.

Watch for hints to assess your likelihood of acquiring a property. For example, if the bank had begun with an Asking Price of $80,000 and had lowered the price only once over the course of the five months to $75,000, then logic tells you that this is one stubborn bank that refuses to accept the lack of interest for this home. However, if the bank began with an Asking Price of $80,000, lowered it to $70,000, and later lowered it again to $65,000 (as in this example), the Asking Price is now within $10,500 of your Maximum Purchase Price. In this case, the seller has shown a propensity to reduce the price to sell the house and your chances of buying it at your Maximum Purchase Price are improved.

Keep in mind that the Buy and Lease/Purchase strategy has six profit sources, so even if the costs associated with fixing up the property exceeded the $15,000 repair and improvement allotment and cut into your $23,000 Total Investor Discount, you can still realize substantial profits from the other five profit sources associated with this lease/purchase strategy. Good strategies allow you flexibility so if things don't go according to plan, you'll still make solid profit.

No matter how careful you are, real estate has its share of surprises. If you invest in real estate in any significant manner, you'll certainly experience some of them. Sometimes the surprises are good and other times they're not. The bottom line is that the Buy and Lease/Purchase strategy, with the six profit sources, positions you to profit consistently.

Example 2: The Bullied Condo

In this example, you're considering purchasing a condominium unit; comparable condominiums in the community in good condition sell for $100,000. After being on the market for six months, this condo is being sold at a real estate auction by a bank that took it back as a postforeclosure. Because the condo was foreclosed on, the previous owners took out their anger on the condo. They broke windows, spray painted walls, and ruined the carpet. You estimate repairs to this property at $6,000. You also notice that the view from several windows is partially obstructed by a sign. Other than the broken windows, the exterior is in great condition and the condo is in one of the top condominium complexes in the community. As the investor, you choose the Buy and Flip strategy.

To begin calculating the Maximum Purchase Price, start with the Fair Market Value, which you have determined to be $100,000. The Repair and Improvement Cost is $6,000. The total for all Other Costs is $7,500.

Now you need to determine your Total Investor Discount. First, because you're using the Buy and Flip strategy, the Minimum Investor Discount Percentage will be 20 percent. Next, the repairs and improvements will be $6,000, which is 6 percent of the Fair Market Value. Therefore, the Repair and Improvement Hassle Percentage is 2 percent (6 percent divided by 3). The obstructed view is the only negative attribute and it may not register with many potential buyers. Therefore, you decide that the Negative Property Attributes Percentage should be 1 percent. Finally, because the condo has been on the market for six months, the Length of Time on the Market Percentage is 4 percent (1 percent for every month over two months).

In summary, the Total Investor Discount Percentage is 27 percent (20 percent + 2 percent + 1 percent + 4 percent). Therefore, your Total Investor Discount is $27,000 (27 percent × $100,000). This puts your Maximum Purchase Price at $59,500 ($100,000 – $6,000 – $7,500 – $27,000).

What does all this mean? Because the bank has had this condo for six months, it is probably motivated to sell and start making the money work for it again in the form of a loan. The bank REO manager probably realizes that the condo shows poorly. However, the bank clearly has chosen not to invest any more money into this property. Further evidence is that it has sent this property to auction. Even though the bank will require a minimum bid, it is essentially saying this property will be sold now to the highest bidder.

You have a decent chance of getting a good deal on this property as long as you don't get caught up in the heat of the moment and place a bid at the auction that exceeds your Maximum Purchase Price. If you do go over your Maximum Purchase Price, you put your profit at risk. Remember, you still risk any cost overruns related to repairing the condo or a schedule delay to prepare the condo for sale. Plus, the condo may sell more slowly than anticipated (especially if it has acquired a bad reputation because it was on the market for six months). Also, because you chose the Buy and Flip strategy, you won't recoup any profits with rental or lease/purchase proceeds.

Because the bank is offering this condo for auction rather than for sale, the bank's minimum bid will be even more significant than the price it is asking for on the retail market (it can be either higher or lower.) When you negotiate, there is always the potential to bridge the gap between the seller's Asking Price and your Maximum Purchase Price through negotiations. However, if a property is going to auction and the minimum bid (the auction's Asking Price) exceeds your Maximum Purchase Price, then you probably won't be able to purchase this property at the auction.

If the auction's minimum bid is higher than your Maximum Purchase Price, should you give up on the property? No! You still may have a chance at it. If the bank has placed a minimum bid on this property that is too high a minimum, it may not attract interest at the auction. If it doesn't, then the condo goes back to the bank and you now have two things you can use to your advantage. First, the bank clearly knows that its minimum bid was too high because the property attracted no interest. Second, as soon as the property goes back to the bank, the bank no longer has the cost of the auctioneer's commission associated with disposing of the property. Contact the REO agent or the bank's postforeclosure manager immediately and make an offer.

Example 3: The Forgotten Office Building

Comparable office buildings in the community in good condition sell for $500,000. One of the first built in the community more than 50 years ago, this office building shows its age. Over the years the central business district of this community has shifted and is now a few miles away. There are currently no tenants; the interior needs new paint, carpet, and lighting throughout; the exterior needs a paint job; and the building needs a new roof and heating and air-conditioning system. The building is owned by three brothers who inherited it, debt-free. It's been sitting on the market for one year. The estimate for Repair and Improvement Costs is $100,000 and the estimate for all Other Costs is $20,000. As the investor, you plan to use the Buy and Hold strategy and become a landlord.

Determining the Fair Market Value of the building is tricky because it's not located with most of the other office buildings in the community. Therefore, you'll be conservative and choose $450,000 as the Fair Market Value after all repairs and improvements are complete.

Now you determine your Total Investor Discount. Because you chose the Buy and Hold strategy, you'll use a 5 percent Minimum Investor Discount Percentage. The repairs and improvements are estimated at $100,000, which equates to 22.2 percent of the Fair Market Value of $450,000. Therefore, the Repair and Improvement Hassle Percentage will be 8 percent (22.2 percent divided by 3 and rounded up for a buffer). You may choose to increase the RIH%, but 8 percent will probably adequately compensate you for your time and effort. The building has many negative attributes. You assign a Negative Property Attributes Percentage of 5 percent. Finally, because this property has been on the market for one year, you set the Length of Time on the Market Percentage at 9 percent (1 percent for every month over three months on the market—not two months since it's a commercial property).

Now, let's determine your Total Investor Discount Percentage, Total Investor Discount, and Maximum Purchase Price. (See Figure 5.12.)

Figure 5.12 *Calculations of TID%, TID, and Maximum Purchase Price*

Your Total Investor Discount Percentage is:
> 5% (MID%) + 8% (RIH%) + 5% (NPA%) + 9% (LTM%) = 27%
> The dollar amount of your Total Investor Discount is:
> 27% × $450,000 = $122,000 (rounded up)

Your Maximum Purchase Price is:
> $450,000 – $100,000 – $20,000 – $122,000 = $208,000

Your Total Investor Discount Percentage for the forgotten office building is 27 percent, your Total Investor Discount is $122,000, and your Maximum Purchase Price is $208,000.

Now your Maximum Purchase Price is $208,000, and you might question whether the family would sell this office building to you for this amount. You determined that the Fair Market Value for this building in fixed-up condition is $450,000, and your Maximum Purchase Price is more than a 50 percent discount off this.

Think about the forgotten office building and your Maximum Purchase Price from the family's perspective. This building needs a serious face-lift and isn't in a good location. It's vacant, so it's not generating any income. In fact, due to taxes and insurance, it's probably costing the family money. The family owns the building free and clear so all the sales proceeds will go directly into the brothers' pockets. Finally, family members obviously decided not to sink any money into the building and they've been trying to unload it for a year. If you're willing to take the time, effort, and risk associated with buying this building, then buying the property for your Maximum Purchase Price of $208,000 might be a win-win for you and the family.

Before you make your final decision, analyze the building's monthly payments (mortgage payment, upkeep, etc.) versus its potential monthly rent receipts to ensure this property will have a positive cash flow for the long term, including enough revenue to cover any short-term surprises that would impact your profits. Remember, you're entitled to the 27 percent Total Investor Discount because of the time and effort you'll invest and the risk of getting the building fixed up on time and on budget. Plus, you need to rent the offices to tenants fairly quickly. If any of these plans go offtrack, then your profit, time, and effort could be significantly impacted.

Example 4: The Perfect House That's Not the Perfect Investment

In the previous examples, all the properties needed repairs, which helped us illustrate the different variables in the Maximum Purchase Price formula. Now, how does the Maximum Purchase

Price formula work for the perfect house, that is *not* the perfect investment?

This house is in the same neighborhood as the 1970s house in a ditch. Most of the houses in this neighborhood sell for $100,000. The perfect house is on Tamarshua Lane in the Dafna subdivision. It is owned by Mel and Lucille Weintraub, who have lived in it for ten years with their four children: Ellen, Bonnie, Myles, and Brad. They have treated this house with tender loving care and simply need a larger house now because the kids are growing up. This house is in immaculate condition. The paint and carpet are new, appliances are updated, and the house sits on a large, flat lot nestled in a quiet section of the neighborhood. The Weintraubs just put the house on the market with one of the top real estate agents in the community, Adam David, and they expect the house to sell quickly. Their Asking Price is $100,000.

Neighbors Mala and Moshe Sarah are starting their real estate investing business. They're a married couple looking to invest part-time while they maintain their full-time jobs. They've read many books, including *Buy Even Lower* and *Buy Low, Rent Smart, Sell High,* and are ready to get started. They're eager to buy their first investment property.

The perfect house is in their neighborhood. They know the neighborhood is stable. They've also known the Weintraubs for years and they know the house is in great condition. They also love the proximity of the property, which is close to their house.

When the perfect house goes on the market, they immediately consider it for their first investment property because it seems like the perfect house for them. The Sarahs need to determine their Maximum Purchase Price. The Fair Market Value is $100,000, the house doesn't need repairs or improvements, and they estimate Other Costs to be a mere $3,000.

They start thinking about the Total Investor Discount. Because the house is perfect and has just been put on the market, the Repair and Improvement Hassle, Negative Property Attributes, and Length of Time on the Market Percentages are all zero. Therefore, that leaves the Sarahs with the Minimum Investor Discount

Percentage. First, they consider the Buy and Flip strategy and quickly realize that, with a 20 percent Minimum Investor Discount Percentage, the sellers wouldn't accept their offer. The Sarahs then move to the Buy and Lease/Purchase strategy and realize that the Weintraubs are highly unlikely to agree to discount the property 10 percent just so the Sarahs can profit from the purchase. Next, the Sarahs consider the Buy and Hold strategy. After getting excited about the long-term prospects of owning a nearby home in a stable neighborhood, they remind themselves that the Weintraubs will have no reason to discount the property even 5 percent just so the Sarahs can profit from the house.

The Sarahs attended one of our Buy Even Lower seminars and learned that they need an appropriate Total Investor Discount to support their planned strategy. This house seems perfect for them and they wonder if the Total Investor Discount doesn't apply to their situation. After all, the house is in perfect condition, on a perfect lot, only walking distance from their home, and in a great neighborhood. The Sarahs feel their long-term prospects (the appreciation and the rental income over time) will be satisfactory. Therefore, they decide to use a Minimum Investor Discount Percentage of zero, which puts the Total Investor Discount at zero. They rationalize that the long-term profits will make up for the lack of short-term Total Investor Discount profits.

Next, the Sarahs determine the Maximum Purchase Price. Other Costs are $3,000, leaving them with a Maximum Purchase Price of $97,000 ($100,000 Fair Market Value minus $3,000 in Other Costs).

Would the Weintraubs accept a slightly discounted offer of only $3,000? What if the house isn't so perfect? What if the furnace or air conditioner goes out? What if the roof starts leaking? What if it takes several months to rent the house and they must make several mortgage payments out of their pockets? What if the tenant doesn't take care of the house like the Weintraubs did? What if there is tenant turnover?

The Weintraubs would probably not discount the house immediately. More important, real estate investors rarely, if ever, get guarantees about long-term profits. This is why short-term profits—buying properties at the appropriate discount (Buying Even Lower)—are so important.

With the Buy and Hold and Buy and Lease/Purchase strategies, because you can diversify your profit sources, you can accept smaller Total Investor Discounts. However, if profits are too small on the front end, then you must wait that much longer to realize profits (if ever) on the back end. If the Sarahs pay the Weintraubs' Asking Price, this will preclude them from using the Buy and Flip and Buy and Lease/Purchase strategies. It's important that they thoroughly understand their profit risk before they buy this house as a Buy and Hold investment (they would be taking on a lot more profit risk than most prudent investors would be willing to assume). Yes, this house may be perfect in many ways. However, this perfect house is clearly not the perfect investment, even for the Sarahs.

6

GOLDEN KEY 5—MAKE SOLID OFFERS

If you will be negotiating to buy a property, then your initial offer should play a pivotal role in your ability to Buy Even Lower. However, many investors jump into negotiations without making a solid offer, which can lead to a variety of problems.

If your offer is too low (often called a *lowball offer),* the seller may reject it and come away with a negative, skeptical view of you. This can have a significant ramification if you make another offer. Also, if the seller has multiple properties or is an institutional seller, the damage created by a lowball offer could impair a great future source of discount properties.

On the other hand, if your initial offer is too high, you may not have enough room to negotiate the contract to a successful—and profitable—conclusion. For example, for Golden Key 4, you learned how to determine your Maximum Purchase Price, but as a successful investor, you'd rarely open negotiations with your Maximum Purchase Price.

Most real estate investment purchases take more than one round of negotiations. Negotiations can center on the price or on other key components of the real estate purchase contract, such as requested repairs prior to closing, repair contributions, contributions to closing costs, or financing. Therefore, before you make an initial offer, do your best to understand the key terms of the purchase and how all the components work together to affect the entire deal. Do this, and you'll be better positioned to make an offer at the appropriate price and other key terms.

Consider that up until this stage in your investment process, your time and energy are essentially research or preparatory. But once you make an offer, you're no longer simply assessing and theoretically considering investing in the property. *You're now putting your money on the line.* For many investors, this is a big dose of reality—they submit a paper with their signature and realize they're potentially obligating themselves to commit serious money, time, and effort to buy and manage an investment property. Making the offer can be a stressful time for many investors. By following the steps in this book, we hope you can minimize the stress that comes with negotiating.

Before you make an offer, you need to understand the key financial components. The following describes these and shows you how they work together so you can consistently Buy Even Lower.

ASKING PRICE

The seller's Asking Price gives you an important perspective on your offer. After all, it's essentially the seller's opening offer.

Some purchasers believe the Asking Price is the amount the seller expects to receive for the property. This usually isn't the case, especially if a property has been on the market for several weeks or several months—even if the seller has reduced the Asking Price.

Therefore, when you put together an offer, assess it in the context of the seller's Asking Price and other key points, such as the condition of the property, owner financing offered, and so on. This helps you avoid getting off on the wrong foot with the seller on a perceived lowball offer, positions you with an offer that isn't too high, and allows room for negotiation.

MAXIMUM PURCHASE PRICE

Remember, the Maximum Purchase Price is the most you should pay for the property to make it a successful and profitable investment. Because real estate investment purchases are rarely completed on the terms of the initial offer, it's critical to understand the role the Maximum Purchase Price plays in making the offer.

We suggest *never* using the Maximum Purchase Price in your initial offer. You don't want to start the negotiation there. In fact, it's where you want to *stop* the negotiation. Your Maximum Purchase Price is key to your profit margin as discussed for Golden Key 4.

The Maximum Purchase Price is often referred to by us as the *ceiling price*. Every time you increase your offer during a negotiation, think of it as a balloon rising inside a room. Your final offer—the highest the balloon should go—is the ceiling. Ideally, the negotiations stop before the balloon touches the ceiling (arrives at your Maximum Purchase Price), so you'll receive an even greater Total Investor Discount and more profit.

INITIAL OFFER PRICE

This is the initial price you offer the seller to buy the investment property. Again, your Initial Offer Price should be below your Maximum Purchase Price to start the negotiation.

Think of the Initial Offer Price as your *floor price*—the least you'll get to pay for the property. Although most real estate investment purchases take several rounds of negotiations, sometimes the seller will accept your Initial Offer Price. Once you give the seller your initial offer, you'll have to live with it as your floor price, even if you later feel the seller would have accepted an even lower purchase price. Therefore, carefully consider your Initial Offer Price.

The amount of your Initial Offer Price can make all the difference in whether the negotiations get off to a good start or not. On the one hand, it's your floor price so you don't want to come in too high. On the other hand, if you come in too low, you risk losing credibility with the seller.

Some investors love to use lowball offers. They make a lot of offers and hope some will stick. We recommend you don't use this shotgun approach. These investors usually have little regard for the emotional impact the lowball offer might have on the seller. Additionally, many sellers won't extend a counteroffer, will perceive the investor as a jerk or shark, and decide not to deal with that investor anymore. This is particularly relevant if the seller is a financial institution or the seller's agent is a key real estate agent in the community.

Lowball offers are most often used by investors who buy investment property using these methods: preforeclosures, foreclosures, distressed sellers, real estate auctions, tax liens and deeds, pounding the pavement, and estate sales. With these methods, the investor either makes an offer to a seller whom he or she will probably never do business with again and/or makes offers to institutional sellers who are disposing of property owned by others and have no emotional attachment. (Note that some auctions have a minimum starting bid, which eliminates lowball offers.)

We've made a significant amount of our profit from buying postforeclosure and corporate relocation real estate. We've found that forming relationships is extremely important when consistently purchasing discount property from the same sellers (financial institutions and big corporations) and through key real estate agents (REO and corporate relocation agents). Therefore, if our offers are perceived as lowball offers, we run the risk of getting a new relationship off to a bad start, hurting a good relationship, or ending an important relationship with a seller or seller's agent.

Red-Face Test

Most sellers and agents don't like to deal with investors who seem inexperienced or waste their time with lowball offers. That's why we put every Initial Offer Price through the Red-Face Test. While we want the Initial Offer Price to be a floor price we can live with, we don't want it to be so low that the seller or agent becomes exasperated with us. For the Initial Offer Price to pass the Red-Face Test, we must believe the seller will view it as a fair offer. Frankly, this is one of the most difficult aspects of making a solid offer.

The Red-Face Test
Use the following four-point process to assess whether your Initial Offer Price passes the Red-Face Test.

1. **Put yourself in the shoes of the seller.** If you were the seller, would you take the offer seriously, or would you think it was totally unrealistic and simply a lowball offer? (Later in this chapter, you'll see a cover letter presented with the offer that shows the seller why it's realistic and well thought out.)

2. **Compare the Initial Offer Price to the Asking Price.** If the Initial Offer Price is substantially less than the seller's Asking Price, you risk turning off the seller. Writing a persuasive cover letter can play a significant role in helping the seller see your offer is reasonable.

3. **Keep your Initial Offer Price above key psychological levels.** For example, if your Initial Offer Price is $188,000, consider instead coming in at $190,000. Numbers at the $10,000 (or the $100,000) marks are often psychological points for the seller. Although there is only $2,000 difference between $188,000 and $190,000, there is a disproportional likelihood that the seller will take your offer more seriously.

4. **Talk to the seller or agent.** Explain to the sellers that you're an investor and ask them the amount they'll accept. If you're a new investor, you may feel this question is intrusive and be afraid to ask it,

> **T**he **R**ed-**F**ace **T**est *(continued)*
> but there's no harm trying to gain insight into what the seller is
> thinking. Once you've established a relationship with a seller or
> agent, asking this question becomes easier.

Wiggle-Room Discount

How do you determine an appropriate Initial Offer Price? First, discount the Maximum Purchase Price 5 to 25 percent. This reduction is meant to provide wiggle room in the negotiations, so we call it the Wiggle-Room Discount. For properties that have low Repair and Improvement Costs, few negative properties attributes, and a relatively short length of time on the market, we suggest choosing a Wiggle-Room Discount of 5 to 10 percent. For properties with high Repair and Improvement Costs, multiple negative property attributes, and a relatively long length of time on the market, we suggest applying a Wiggle-Room Discount of at least 15 to 25 percent. Why? The more negatives associated with the property, the more give and take you'll probably experience in the negotiation. The following examples show how to apply the Wiggle-Room Discount when determining the Initial Offer Price.

Example 1: The Job Transfer Sellers

The house at 123 Alpha Street is nearly ready to go on the market. There is nothing wrong with the house. However, the sellers mentioned they want to sell the property quickly because of a job transfer. They received your letter stating that you were an investor. They have not yet listed the home with an agent and are willing to give a reasonable investor discount. The house needs an estimated $10,000 of repairs and has no negative property attributes. The Asking Price is $205,000 and the comps put the property's Fair Market Value at $220,000 in good condition. You plan to Buy and Lease/Purchase this property. You've set your Maximum Purchase Price at $195,000. You've estimated the relatively minor repairs to be less than 5 percent of the Fair Market Value, so you calculate a Wiggle-Room Discount of 5 percent. That would make it $9,750, so you choose the round number of $10,000 for your Wiggle-Room Discount. Remember, your Maximum Purchase Price is $195,000. You present the seller with an Initial Offer Price of $185,000.

Will your Initial Offer Price pass the Red-Face Test? The sellers know you're an investor who needs to make a profit. You explain your rationale in the cover letter that goes with your offer. You hope they'll see that you're sincerely working toward a fair, win-win deal. If they do, then the negotiation will begin and you now have a chance of obtaining the property for between $185,000 (your Initial Offer Price) and $195,000 (your Maximum Purchase Price).

Example 2: The Foreclosed House Needing Repairs

The house at 5860 Pinebrook Road is in a good neighborhood, has been on the market for four months, and requires involved repairs and significant improvements estimated to cost $30,000. A bank took the house back in a foreclosure and apparently doesn't want to spend more money on it. Additionally, this house has a slight negative property attribute in that the yard is 25 percent smaller than those of neighboring houses. The Asking Price is $150,000 and, fixed up, its Fair Market Value in good condition is $200,000 to $220,000. You choose $200,000 to be on the safe side. If you buy the property, you plan to employ the Buy and Lease/Purchase strategy for this house. After you assess the repairs and improvements while taking into consideration the negative property attribute and length of time on the market, you set your Maximum Purchase Price at $135,000.

Next, you need to determine your Initial Offer Price. The repairs and improvements—15 percent of the Fair Market Value—will be more expensive and time-consuming than basic cosmetics such as carpet and paint. Plus, this house has a minor negative home attribute, which you can emphasize in the negotiation process. Because it hasn't been on the market for an extended period of time (only four months), you decide on a 20 percent Wiggle-Room Discount—$27,000. Remember, the Asking Price is $150,000 and your Maximum Purchase Price is $135,000. Therefore, your Initial Offer Price is $108,000. After thinking this over, you believe the psychological price point of $110,000 would pass the Red-Face Test and could make a big difference in the seller taking your offer seriously. Therefore, you choose $110,000 as your Initial Offer Price; your cover letter to the seller explains your rationale.

To some, this may seem like a lowball offer because the bank is asking $150,000. Additionally, an Initial Offer Price of $110,000 is almost one-third off the current Asking Price and nearly a 50 percent discount off the Fair Market Value of the house in good condition. However, this house is in bad condition and isn't selling. You can assume the bank knows this house may sit a long time, and it needs to get its money out of that house and working for it again. Therefore, your odds are good that they will not be offended by the offer.

REAL ESTATE PURCHASE CONTRACT

Once you understand the key financial concepts to make solid offers, it's time to make the offer. Always submit offers in a written real estate purchase contract. You should also understand all of the provisions in this legal document before affixing your signature to it.

As an investor, you have a variety of real estate purchase contracts you can use. This chapter presents a sample contract you can use to buy single-family houses. Have your real estate attorney look over any legal document you intend to use; each state has specific laws and issues that necessitate certain clauses. The real estate purchase contract included here is specifically geared toward the business strategy of buying postforeclosure single-family houses. You may need to modify the terms to meet the specifics of your investment preference and location.

Sample Real Estate Purchase Contract

In this sample real estate purchase contract, provisions A through G are the general provisions found in most real estate purchase contracts. Provisions H through O are special provisions specific to the purchaser's particular interests.

> **A. PURCHASE AND SALE OF PROPERTY.** The undersigned purchaser agrees to buy, and the undersigned seller agrees to sell all that tract of land, with such improvements as are located thereon, described as follows: The house known as _____ according to the present system of numbering. Together with all lighting fixtures attached thereto, all electrical, mechanical, plumbing, air-conditioning, and any other systems or fixtures as are attached thereto; all television antennas and mailboxes; and all plants, trees, and shrubbery now a part of the property. The full legal description of said property is the same as is recorded with the clerk of the superior court of the county in which the property is located and is made a part of this agreement by reference.

The *purchase and sale of property* provision specifies the commitment of the seller to sell and the purchaser to purchase the property. Place the physical address of the property in the blank space. Note that the property includes everything attached to the property, such as lights, heating, air-conditioning, and plant life. If you want to be even more careful, are buying undeveloped land, or are buying land not commonly known by a physical address (such as 1234 Dodick Drive), then you'll need to include the legal description of the property to properly identify it. You can also attach a survey to a purchase contract as an addendum. You don't want to obligate yourself to purchase a different property or smaller lot than you thought you were getting.

> **B. PURCHASE PRICE AND METHOD OF PAYMENT.**
> The purchase price of the property shall be: _____
> dollars. Purchase is contingent on purchaser obtaining an
> investor loan at __% down payment with an interest rate
> not to exceed __% on a __-year loan.

The *purchase price and method of payment* provision specifies both the sales price for the property and any financing contingency. When you make the initial offer, the purchase price will be the Initial Offer Price. If the offer is not contingent on financing or is all cash, then remove this financing sentence. In fact, if you simply cross out this sentence and add "This offer is not contingent on financing," it reinforces to the seller that your offer has fewer contingencies than many other offers. In the seller's eyes, this reduces the probability of things going wrong after acceptance of the offer and gives them confidence that you're more likely to follow through with the purchase.

When you use the contingent financing sentence, be sure to specify the term and interest rate of the loan you plan to secure. If this loan becomes unobtainable (for example, you lose your job and can't qualify for the loan), you're no longer obligated to buy this property. As discussed for Golden Key 1, understand your financial resources in advance and have a lender lined up before you make any offers. Most loans allow you to lock in the terms for 60 days; prudent investors immediately lock in their financing once the contract is fully accepted.

Remember that cash is often the most limiting factor in building a real estate portfolio. Again, *cash is king*. Therefore, pay particular attention to growing your cash and making it go as far as possible. One way is to select a low down payment. When we first started our partnership in the early 1990s, most investment loan products available required down payments of 25 percent or more. We didn't have that kind of cash to buy many homes.

Today, you can find good investor loans with down payments of as little as 10 percent. The differential in terms (such as the interest rate and term of the loan) between a 10 and 20 percent down payment investor loan may be insignificant depending on the interest rate of the loan. Therefore, you may not be hurting yourself by securing a 10 percent down payment investor loan. However, if you can put down 20 percent or show that you have 20 percent equity in the property, many loans allow you to get out of paying thousands of dollars (usually spread out over the term of the loan) in private mortgage insurance (PMI), which is often required when owners finance more than 80 percent of the appraised value of residential property.

If you buy from a financial institution and hope to obtain in-house financing or believe an individual may be willing to offer owner financing, insert a sentence requesting the financing in this clause. By obtaining owner financing from a financial institution or individual, you may (though not always) obtain better terms and save on finance costs.

C. EARNEST MONEY. Purchaser has paid to the undersigned seller, _____ ($), receipt whereof is hereby acknowledged as earnest money, and is to be applied as part of payment of purchase price of said property at the time of closing. Purchaser and seller agree that the seller shall deposit earnest money in the seller's account by the third banking day following acceptance of this agreement by all parties; all parties have agreed that said escrow/trust account will be an interest-bearing account, with interest also applied to the purchase price at the time of closing. The parties to this contract understand and acknowledge that disbursement of earnest moneys held by the escrow agent can occur only at closing; upon written agreement signed by all parties having an interest in the funds; upon court order; or upon failure of loan approval; or as otherwise set out herein. This contract is voidable at seller's option if the earnest money check is not paid when presented to the drawee bank.

The *earnest money* provision specifies both the amount and conditions by which the earnest money is presented by the purchaser to the seller or seller's agent. Be careful with the amount to agree to for the earnest money. If you need to walk away from the property after you've signed the contract and have paid your earnest money, the seller may try to keep some or all of it. Your justification for getting your earnest money back should be covered with one of the contingency provisions contained within this purchase contract. The inability to obtain financing, unexpected problems with the house, and a surprise lien are common contingency provisions.

Sellers can sometimes react negatively when the buyer exercises a contingency provision. Therefore, even if you exercise the contingency legally, sellers sometimes make the process of returning your earnest money difficult. Spending the time and money to pursue legal action may not be worth it. Therefore, it's better to provide as small an amount of earnest money as reasonable. A rule of thumb is $1,000 of earnest money for every $100,000 of property sales price. If the seller perceives that you represent a risk of defaulting on the contract, he or she may press you for more earnest money. Conversely, if you are buying from an institutional seller and have established a reputation as a reliable investor, you may be able to commit to less earnest money due to the benefits that come with familiarity and credibility.

D. WARRANTY OF TITLE. Seller warrants that he or she presently has title to said property, and at time of closing, agrees to convey good and marketable title to said property to purchaser by general warranty deed subject only to (1) zoning ordinances affecting said property, (2) general utility easements of record serving said property, (3) sub-division restrictions of record, and (4) leases, other ease-ments, other restrictions and encumbrances specified in this contract.

The *warranty of title* provision protects the purchaser in the event that the seller is attempting (willingly or unwillingly) to sell a property in which he or she doesn't have a good and marketable title. The closing attorney or a title company (depending on the laws of the particular state) should perform a title examination before the closing to confirm a good and marketable title. Addi-tionally, buyers should purchase title insurance due to any error related to the examination, such as inaccurate county records, searcher error, attorney review error, and so on.

E. TITLE EXAMINATION. The purchaser shall have a reasonable time after acceptance of this contract to exam-ine the title and furnish seller with a written statement of objections affecting the marketability of said title. Seller shall have a reasonable time, after receipt of such objec-tions, to satisfy all valid objections, and if seller fails to sat-isfy such valid objections within a reasonable time, then at the option of the purchaser, evidenced by written notice to seller, this contract shall be null and void. Marketable title as used herein shall mean title which a title insurance company licensed to do business in the state of _____ will insure at its regular rates, subject only to standard ex-ceptions unless otherwise specified herein.

The *title examination* provision clarifies the purchaser's right to examine the title. This provision works together with the warranty of title provision. As mentioned earlier, the title search is generally conducted by either the closing attorney or the title company. Again, be sure to take out title insurance with any purchase of real estate. Even the most conscientious attorney or title company can miss a detail. Having title insurance will protect you if a title issue arises after the purchase is completed at closing. If you question the value of title insurance, remember that just one significant title problem could pay for many dozens of title insurance policies.

F. CONDITION OF PREMISES. Seller warrants that at the time of closing, the premises will be in the same condition as it is on the date that this contract is signed by the seller, normal wear and tear excepted. However, should the premises be destroyed or substantially damaged before the time of closing, then at the election of the purchaser: (a) the contract may be canceled, or (b) the purchaser may consummate the contract and receive such insurance as is paid on the claim of loss. This election is to be exercised within 10 days after the purchaser has been notified in writing by the seller of the amount of the insurance proceeds, if any, the seller will receive on the claim of loss. If the purchaser hasn't been so notified within 45 days, subsequent to the occurrence of such damage or destruction, purchaser may, at its option, cancel the contract.

The *condition of premises* provision prevents the seller from damaging or neglecting the property prior to closing. This provision protects the buyer if the property incurs significant damage between the time the contract is completely signed by all the parties and the time of closing. This is an important provision if the property is occupied by the seller after the contract has been agreed to and up until closing. This provision may also come into play in areas prone to hurricanes, tornadoes, earthquakes, wildfires, mudslides, and so on.

G. RESPONSIBILITY TO COOPERATE. Seller and purchaser agree that such documents as may be necessary to carry out the terms of this contract shall be produced, executed, and/or delivered by such parties at the time required to fulfill the terms and conditions of this agreement.

The *responsibility to cooperate* provision legally binds all parties to sign the appropriate paperwork to complete the terms of the contract. It also legally obligates both parties to do this in a timely manner.

H. REAL ESTATE TAXES. Real estate taxes on said property for the calendar year in which the sale is closed shall be prorated as of the date of closing.

The *real estate taxes* provision clarifies that you are obligated to pay taxes due from the date of purchase. Therefore, the seller is contractually bound to pay all taxes up to the purchase date. Because real estate taxes for the full year are often paid by the seller (prior to the closing) or by the buyer (after the closing), at the closing, a prorated amount is usually given to the party who has paid or will pay the taxes.

I. STATE TRANSFER TAX. Seller shall pay state of _____ property transfer tax.

You only should use the *state transfer tax* provision in states that require a transfer tax upon the sale of real estate. In states that require it, the seller customarily pays the tax.

J. CLOSING DATE AND COSTS. Sale shall be closed on or before _____ at such time, date, and location specified by the seller. Seller shall pay all closing costs, including attorney fees, loan fees, and processing fees in connection with the sale of the subject property to the purchaser.

The *closing date and costs* provision obligates both parties to close by a specific date. The closing date is important because it sets the amount of time you'll have to arrange your financing or risk losing the property and your earnest money. Sellers often want to close quickly. Because of the challenges often associated with loans, 30 to 60 days is the typical, acceptable range. As a purchaser, ask for a closing date as far out as reasonable.

Closing costs can range from paying attorney fees only to paying attorney fees, loan fees, processing fees, and more. Clearly, closing costs can materially affect your offer. Asking the seller to pay all the closing costs will usually not severely turn off the seller from your offer. On the other hand, closing costs tend to be one of the most negotiated terms in the contract. You may end up paying some or all of the closing costs, depending on the other terms of the purchase. Some investors agree to put a cap in the contract, such as "seller to pay closing costs, not to exceed $5,000."

Remember that the Maximum Purchase Price formula includes Legal Costs and Finance Costs as components of the Other Costs category. Therefore, if you can get the seller to pay all or some of these costs, be sure to make the appropriate adjustment to your Maximum Purchase Price. In other words, when your Other Costs decrease, your Maximum Purchase Price can increase by the same amount.

> **K. UTILITY BILL PRORATED.** Seller and purchaser agree to prorate between themselves, as of the date of closing, any and all utility bills rendered subsequent to closing which include service for any period of time the property was owned by the seller or any prior owner.

The same logic that applies to the real estate taxes provision applies to the *utility bill prorated* provision. The seller pays all utilities to the property up to the day of closing and the purchaser starts paying the utilities after the closing date.

L. WOOD INFESTATION REPORT. At the time of closing the seller shall provide the purchaser with a wood-destroying infestation report, in the current form officially approved by _____ structural pest control commission, from a properly licensed pest control company stating that the main dwelling has been inspected and found to be free of visible infestation and structural damage caused by termites and other wood-destroying organisms or that, if such infestation or structural damage existed, it has been corrected. The inspection referred to in such report shall have been made within 30 days prior to closing. The inspection and termite letter is to be provided by _____.

The *wood infestation report* provision needs to be specific to the laws and regulations of your state. In the first blank space, add your state or jurisdiction. For example, in Georgia, a seller can't sell real property without producing a termite letter at closing.

Keep in mind that successful real estate investing is about attention to detail. We have worked with a termite and pest control company for many years. We trust their work and their advice. They have discovered hidden termite issues that helped us avoid buying money pits. The second blank space in this provision allows us to specify that the termite letter will be provided by our termite company.

Generally, the seller has the right to select the company to provide the termite letter and many financial institutions have a preset arrangement with a specific company. However, there are two big reasons that you should push to use your preferred termite company in the contract. First, this gives you the assurance that the termite report will properly and fully protect your interest. After all, not all termite companies provide the same level of quality in their inspections. Our termite company once found many costly issues that the seller's original termite company had missed. Fortunately, we had our termite company perform an inspection before closing on the property. This seemingly small item turned into a big cost saver.

Second, we maintain a termite bond on all of our properties until they are sold. Therefore, with our termite company writing the termite letter for the closing, they are now set up to write the renewable bond on the property for as long as we own it. That way, we avoid paying for another required inspection before a termite company will issue a renewable bond on our property.

> **M. SURVIVAL OF TERMS OF CONTRACT.** Any condition or stipulation of the contract not fulfilled at the time of closing shall survive the closing, execution, and delivery of the warranty deed until such time as said conditions or stipulations are fulfilled. [The closing attorney is directed to transfer this paragraph to the closing statement.]

The *survival of terms of contract* provision protects both parties in case one aspect of the contract is not satisfied at closing. Because closing documents often don't cover every word of the contract and the purchaser usually has to sign many documents at closing (especially if a new loan is being taken out), then neither party has to worry that a word, term, or provision is missing from the closing documents because of this provision.

> **N. SEWER/SEPTIC TANK.** Seller warrants that the main dwelling on the above described property is served by:
>
>   *A PUBLIC SEWER_____
>   OR
>   *A SEPTIC TANK_____
>   (PURCHASER) (SELLER)

The *sewer/septic tank* provision ensures you know what you're getting because sewers and septic tanks are usually hidden. Some investors avoid buying properties with septic tanks because they can cause costly problems. For a property listed with a real estate agent, a seller's property disclosure form, required in many states, also specifies whether a property is served by a sewer or septic tank. Both the seller and purchaser should initial this provision.

O. WALK-THROUGH AND INSPECTION. Purchaser has the right to walk-through the property and to have an inspection of the premises made by a qualified building inspector within 10 business days of acceptance of this contract. Expense of the inspection shall be paid by the purchaser. Should purchaser present to seller within this 10-day period a report citing any deficiencies in the property found during the walk-through or inspection, seller, at his or her option, may elect to correct said deficiencies, request the purchaser to accept "as is," or allow the purchaser to declare the contract null and void. Seller shall have 48 hours to decide which repairs, if any, are to be made. Purchaser shall have 48 hours after notice from the seller to accept the seller's offer of repairs or declare the contract null and void.

The *walk-through and inspection* provision is one of the most important clauses to you as the purchaser. This provision allows you to make an offer and negotiate a contract without first performing a thorough inspection of the property. You then reserve the right to conduct a thorough inspection within ten days after the contract is fully signed. Ten days is usually enough time for you to schedule an inspector without causing the seller to have to wait too long to find out whether the purchaser will come back with a problem found during the inspection.

This provision is extremely important to both the investor and the seller. Sellers often want this inspection completed as quickly as possible so they can move on and consider other offers if problems with the property cause your contract to fall through. *We always hold firmly when negotiating this provision. We don't want to buy an investment with significant hidden problems.* At the same time, we try to reassure the seller that we're only looking for big problems—we're not trying to nickel-and-dime anyone. We also tell them we'll try to have the inspection completed well in advance of the ten days specified—we try to do it.

Notice that this provision is called "walk-through and inspection" rather than "inspection" alone. Many real estate purchase contracts allow the purchaser the right to resubmit the offer or withdraw from the contract if additional problems are found during the inspection. However, you want the right to resubmit or withdraw even if you or your contractor notice something in an informal walk-through. On occasion, we have chosen *not* to get a formal inspection and save some money, which this provision allows.

We recommend quickly scheduling an inspection after the contact is signed. You can identify a qualified building inspector before making the offer on the property. However, it might take a week to get on the inspector's schedule. In addition, the inspector may take a few days to complete a report, especially if he or she has to research an item or get a tool for a more through assessment.

When you determined the Maximum Purchase Price for a given property, presumably you factored in the cost of visible problems. However, if the inspection turns up problems you weren't aware of at the time you extended your offer, you may need to use some of this time to assess the cost to fix the problem. This is especially important when dealing with financial institutions that are your repeat sources of inventory. Your intent is not to nickel-and-dime sellers with small problems after the contract is signed; you only want to go back to them with large, costly issues. It might take time to determine whether a problem found during the inspection is, indeed, large and costly. (For Golden Key 6: Negotiate Like a Chess Master, you'll learn how to handle problems found during the inspection and the tricky skill of reopening negotiations.)

Also, you'll want the inspection to be completed quickly because, if you use an investor loan for the purchase, the loan origination process generally takes several weeks. With most loans requiring nonrefundable application fees, you don't want to pay these until you're relatively certain the purchase will go through. That's why it's important to complete the inspection and any additional negotiations before you pay the application fee and start the loan process.

You'll find the entire sample contract in the Appendix, or download a *free* editable copy at *www.RegularRiches.com/Contract.*

In some cases, after negotiations are complete, financial institutions request (or have a policy) that you transfer the terms to their contract or their real estate agent's contract before they finally sign off. They may have agreed to the key terms of the purchase but didn't take time to carefully read your contract. If these sellers insist on using theirs, carefully review it and ensure that it includes all the provisions that cover your interests. If it doesn't, you may find yourself more negotiations. Work with your attorney to determine which provisions you need to negotiate and which ones you can live with. Be careful; by reopening the negotiations with a financial institution, you may be harming a profitable, long-term relationship.

Making the **C**ontract **L**egally **B**inding

When you sign the contract and submit it with your earnest money to the seller or agent, the offer becomes legally binding on you. In other words, you'll be legally bound to follow through on all the purchaser provisions if the contract is accepted "as is" by the seller within the period you set (typically 24 to 48 hours).

If the seller changes the contract before signing it (such as adjusting the purchase price, closing costs, etc.), then it's not legally binding on you. To make it so, you need to initial all of the changes on the contract, which confirms your acceptance of the seller's changes. This works the same way for any additional changes you make. Therefore, when negotiations for a contract that's been heavily negotiated are complete, you may want to carefully write all the agreed-to terms on a clean real estate purchase contract and have both parties sign the clean contract. This creates a document that everyone, including the closing attorney, can easily read and use.

Some financial institutions work with faxed copies and without earnest money until the deal is finalized. They may not abide by the 24- to 48-hour deadline you've set because the fax process is less formal. However, once both parties finalize the deal, original signatures on the real estate purchase contract and exchanging earnest money are required to make the contract legally binding on all parties. We suggest trying to do this as quickly as you can to lock in your deal.

COVER LETTER

You found a great potential investment property, determined the key financial terms, and completed the real estate purchase contract. You're about to make a solid offer on this investment property. Your Initial Offer Price is considerably less than the seller's Asking Price, but it passes the Red-Face Test and gives you enough wiggle room for a few rounds of negotiations before you top out at your Maximum Purchase Price.

Instead of simply submitting the offer in the real estate purchase contract and waiting for a response, take time to prepare and include a cover letter. This *critical step* may make the difference in whether the seller agrees to the best terms possible—or even agrees to negotiate with you at all.

Your cover letter summarizes for the seller (and his or her real estate agent if the seller has one) the major components in your real estate purchase contract and your rationale behind your offer price and terms. The cover letter cuts through the legal jargon, acts as a road map, and emphasizes the terms that are important to the seller. It also briefly describes why your Initial Offer Price is lower than the Asking Price and why the seller should view your offer as reasonable and acceptable.

How does the cover letter make a huge difference in your ability to Buy Even Lower? First, your cover letter gives you *credibility*. If you've never dealt with the seller and/or agent before, he or she will see that you're making a thoughtful, forthright offer to purchase. The seller may not agree with everything in the cover letter. However, he or she will see that you're a serious professional and that you'll probably follow through to purchase the property if all the parties agree on the contract terms. Also, you separate yourself from the many investors who submit large numbers of lowball offers with little thought.

Second, the cover letter provides *emotional support* as it helps your offer pass the Red-Face Test. With it being lower than the Asking Price, your cover letter connects all the dots so the seller doesn't have to figure out the basis for your offer. Even though the seller may not agree with your terms or logic, he or she should view your offer as fair and reasonable. *Again, the primary goal of the offer is to get the negotiations rolling and not turn off the seller's interest in you as a buyer.*

Third, your cover letter provides *clarity* as it walks them through the key points on one easy-to-read page. Few sellers or agents are willing to read through the entire contract to understand it, then take time to fully assess why your offer might be acceptable or, at least, fair. They'd probably scan the contract you submit and draw quick conclusions. In doing so, they may miss a key term in the contract and almost certainly won't fully appreciate the rationale for your offer.

Fourth, it serves as a *script* for the agent representing the seller. Instead of reading your contract and then trying to summarize key points for the seller, the agent can rely on your cover letter, saving time and effort. More important, by relying on your cover letter as a script, the agent accurately summarizes your key points—and tells the seller a story (your story) that reflects positively on your offer.

Fifth, there is nothing personal about a real estate purchase contract. The cover letter is your *personal, primary means of communication* with the seller. In fact, if you're dealing with an agent, you may never speak with the actual seller. In most states, agents are contractually bound to present to the ultimate seller any offer they receive in writing. We know many of our offers are presented by the listing agent to the seller with our cover letter. Therefore, we feel we gain an advantage because we're communicating directly with the ultimate decision maker through our cover letter.

Sixth, your cover letter serves as a *reference document* during the negotiation process. Negotiations can take days, weeks, or months—you, the seller (e.g., financial institutions), and the agent may also be dealing with many properties. All parties can use the cover letter to keep track of the particulars during the negotiation. Indeed, there's a positive, psychological impact on the sellers when they see the offer and other terms during the negotiation process *summarized* on a single, easy-to-read page.

Finally, it serves as a stated *timeline*. A powerful psychological impact is made when the seller receives your cover letter again and again as you make the same offer on a property over the course of several days, weeks, or months. Sellers consider taking your offer more seriously when your cover letter reminds them how long they've been sitting on that property. (You'll learn more about this negotiation strategy and others for Golden Key 6.)

Key Components of the Cover Letter

The cover letter should be no more than one page long. It should

- start out on a positive note by giving a compliment on the property (if appropriate), thanking the seller for considering your offer, and saying how this is a good property for your investment formula;
- accentuate the negative property attributes to put your offer into proper perspective;
- briefly explain why your offer is a win-win for everyone;
- describe why the Initial Offer Price is lower than the Asking Price, yet is still reasonable;
- show the seller how you mathematically arrived at your Initial Offer Price; and
- tell the seller you can help him or her by purchasing the property quickly and "as is."

The sellers may not agree with your terms and logic. However, they'll likely feel your offer is forthright and well thought out. If they don't agree with any of your estimates, you can adjust these during negotiations as you move from your Initial Offer Price to your Maximum Purchase Price. One number you should include is your Total Investor Discount, though you may want to call it simply the *investor discount*. This reminds the sellers that you need to make a reasonable profit for your time and effort. The Total Investor Discount is also one of the easiest variables to adjust to show the seller you're willing to cut into your profits to make the deal work.

Sample Cover Letters

The following are examples of various cover letters. The first two build off the wiggle-room examples discussed earlier.

Sample 1: The Job Transfer Sellers. It can be difficult to purchase houses directly from individuals because they often have an emotional attachment to their property, which makes it difficult to make discounted offers to them. They often know how much homes sell for in their neighborhood and they can quickly jump to the conclusion that your fair offer is a lowball offer. On the other hand, summarizing the situation in the cover letter will improve your odds of the seller taking your offer seriously. In this example, you're working directly with the sellers who are moving due to a job transfer and, assuming you have direct contact with the sellers, you'd also probably take the time to orally explain your offer.

In this example, the sellers' Asking Price is $205,000, so $15,000 seems to be their estimate for needed repairs because the Fair Market Value of the property in good condition is $220,000. In reality, you believe the repairs can be completed for only $10,000, but $15,000 gives you a buffer.

Your Initial Offer Price is $185,000 and your Maximum Purchase Price is $195,000. You hope the sellers take your offer seriously, recognize an opportunity to sell quickly, and contact you with a counteroffer. When the sellers add up their expenses—repairs, mortgage payments, utility costs, real estate commissions, and miscellaneous costs—it will probably cost them about $35,000 to prepare the house for sale, then sell the house (assuming it will take a few months to sell). They're also trying to sell in December, which is typically a difficult time of year to sell real estate. Therefore, you hope that they contact you with a reasonable amount in a counteroffer and that you can then quickly negotiate to buy the property at or below $195,000.

Date: December 15, 2006
To: Loren and Stephanie Weaver
From: Andy Investor

Re: 123 Alpha Street, Cleveland, OH

Dear Mr. and Mrs. Weaver,

You have a nice house at 123 Alpha Street and I am interested in purchasing it. I know you want to sell it quickly so you can put it behind you and move to California. I also know you are concerned about trying to sell your house during one of the slowest times of the year. As an investor, I can make this happen.

Though my offer may be somewhat lower than you anticipated, it should be a "win-win" for everyone. You will avoid the costs associated with repairing the property, estimated at close to $15,000. You will also avoid extra mortgage payments, utilities, etc., while you try to sell your house during the winter. You won't need to pay 6 percent (approximately $12,000) in real estate commissions if you list the property with an agent. I assume the costs could easily add up to approximately $35,000, in which you would net $185,000 or less. My offer allows you a fair, quick deal that allows you to move to California without the stress associated with selling the house from a distance.

Here's how I arrived at my offer:

Fair Market Value:	$220,000
Repair Costs:	(15,000)
Holding and Misc. Costs:	(8,000)
Real estate agent:	(12,000)
Purchase "Now" and "As Is" offer:	$185,000

Sincerely,

Andy Investor
(contact information)

In this sample cover letter, we try to show the seller how the property will probably net the same amount of money with or without us. We hope the quick sale and reduction of stress will sway the seller. We also choose to leave out any discussion of an investor discount (like we do with financial institutions) because we'd risk confusing the seller. We simply try to walk the seller through the analysis from his or her perspective.

Sample 2: The Foreclosed House Needing Repairs. This property presents an exciting possibility. ABC Bank is sitting on the property and tying up the bank's money. The bank's Asking Price is $150,000 and, with needed repairs costing approximately $30,000, the Fair Market Value is $200,000 to $210,000. Marcy Brian, the bank's REO manager, probably isn't happy with this situation. She has chosen not to fix up the house, has had it listed for months (which is not unreasonable for a house needing this many repairs), and is now entering the fall period when house sales significantly slow down.

Because the seller (the bank) is using a real estate agent, this cover letter uses a different tactic. In this case, you would simply try to walk the REO manager and agent through your analysis from your perspective. We suggest you use the low-end estimate of the Fair Market Value, include a $10,000 buffer for repairs and improvements (bringing them up to $40,000), and include your holding and miscellaneous costs (say $10,000). Also, show them your Total Investor Discount (20 percent to do all the repairs and length of time on the market plus some buffer built in).

All of these numbers are important to create the Wiggle-Room Discount between your Initial Offer Price of $110,000 and the Maximum Purchase Price of $135,000. If Ms. Brian's counteroffer points out that the Fair Market Value is actually $210,000, you can tell her that you'll give her the benefit of the doubt and raise the numbers in your analysis (you can do this because you built this wiggle room into your analysis). The same holds true with the repairs and improvements and holding and miscellaneous costs if Ms. Brian argues strongly that your estimates are too high. If she doesn't make these points but you still need to raise the offer price in the next round of negotiations, you can then simply reduce the Total Investor Discount to show that you'll take less profit to complete the negotiations.

In summary, the Fair Market Value of the property in good condition is $200,000; the bank's Asking Price is $150,000; your Maximum Purchase Price is $135,000; and your Initial Offer Price is $110,000. You hope the bank will take your offer seriously and make a counteroffer of $145,000 or below. From there, you hope to negotiate the purchase at or below your Maximum Purchase Price.

Date: September 25, 20XX
To: Marcy Brian (ABC Bank) and Ellen Barry (Real Estate Agent)
Fax: 123-456-7890
From: Scott Denny
Re: 5860 Pinebrook Road, Atlanta, GA

Dear Ms. Brian and Ms. Barry,

Thank you for considering my offer. This is the type of problem property that usually works well for me as an investor. I know you've had it listed for four months and are now entering the fall "slow down" period for real estate buying. The property requires a significant number of repairs and it's on a smaller lot than most in the neighborhood. These issues are probably a big part of the reason the property hasn't sold. I believe my offer is a win-win and I'm ready to buy the home now and in as-is condition.

The following briefly sets forth the rationale for my offer:

Fair Market Value (in fixed-up condition):	$200,000
Repairs and Improvement Costs:	(40,000)
Holding and Misc. Costs:	(10,000)
Investor Discount (20 percent of Fair Market Value):	(40,000)
Purchase "As Is" offer:	$110,000

Subject to thorough inspection within 10 business days. Offer expires September 27, 20XX.

Sincerely,

Scott Denny
(contact information)

In this sample cover letter, we address it to both the seller and the agent involved to establish a line of communication with them. We start with a positive, touch on the problems with the property, remind them that we're looking for a win-win, and can act fast buying "as is." Finally, we show them how we arrived at our Initial Offer Price. We hope that this is enough to get the negotiations started.

Sample 3: The Worn-Out Duplex. This ugly and awful property has the potential to be a beautiful investment. However, because of its poor condition, the duplex has been sitting on the market for many months.

Here, the seller's Asking Price is $170,000. It's probably worth $200,000 in good condition. You have determined a Maximum Purchase Price of $155,000 and set your Initial Offer Price at $140,000. You estimate repairs to be $25,000, and you build in a $5,000 buffer to bring it to $30,000. Holding and closing costs will probably be $3,000, and with a buffer you set them at $3,600.

Date: January 25, 20XX
To: Austin Addison (XYZ Bank) and Olivia Jack (REO agent)
From: Caroline Dylan
Fax: 123-456-7890
Re: 458 Watson Drive, Cooper Subdivision

Dear Mr. Addison and Ms. Jack,

This property fits my investment formula nicely. The only problem is the current Asking Price is a little high. However, I feel we are close enough that we can reach a fair compromise. Below, I will point out some key points for you to consider.

This duplex has been on the market for some time and hasn't attracted attention at $170,000. I believe this is due to several factors. The repairs are estimated to be $30,000. One significant problem is the roof, as evidenced by the large water stains on the master bedroom ceiling and along the back wall of the house. Further, the HVAC system, while functional, appears to be on its last leg. It will undoubtedly take several months to get this property in shape to market, so there will also be considerable holding costs.

I believe my offer is a win-win. I can act fast and take this problem property off your hands quickly and I'd make what I hope you'd agree as a reasonable investor profit of 12 percent at the same time.

My analysis of 458 Watson Drive follows:

Fair Market Value (in fixed-up condition):	$200,000
Repairs:	(30,000)
Holding and Misc. Costs:	(6,000)
Investor Discount (12 percent of Fair Market Value):	(24,000)
Purchase "As Is" offer:	$140,000

Subject to thorough inspection within 10 business days of acceptance.

Offer expires 1/27/XX.

Sincerely,

Caroline Dylan
(contact information)

Again, we address the cover letter to both the seller and the agent to establish (or maintain) a line of communication with them. As in the previous letter, we start on a positive note, summarize the problems, let then know we want a win-win situation, list the particulars to arrive at our offer price, and remind them that we can close quickly and purchase it "as is." We hope we make a solid enough offer to get the negotiations off to a good start.

Sample 4: The Neglected Office Building. Just like for residential properties, we suggest you use a cover letter for commercial properties. The Fair Market Value of this office building in good condition is $300,000. The seller's Asking Price is $200,000, which shows that he or she realizes the property needs significant repairs and improvements. Therefore, you choose an Initial Offer Price of $160,000 to get the negotiations rolling and aim to purchase the property at or below your Maximum Purchase Price of $180,000. You plan to use the Buy and Hold strategy, so your Total Investor Discount is only 10 percent—you'll make most of your profits on this office building through long-term tenant rents.

Date: October 8, 20XX

To: James Riseman (REO agent) and Joe Henles (Big Bank Corp.)

From: Sonal Patel

Re: 2846 David Street, Jonesboro, GA 32005

Dear Mr. Riseman and Mr. Henles,

Following is my offer, summarized below, regarding your office building at 2846 David Street. This building has a lot of potential. However, there are a few key points I wish to emphasize.

First, the commercial rental market in this community seems to be slowing down, with office building values seeming to follow this downward trend. Second, the building needs approximately $100,000 in repairs/improvements. All carpeting needs to be replaced and the interior needs to be painted. There appears to be some termite damage on the exterior west side of the building.

I know you are asking $200,000 for the building. However, the repairs and improvements may take somewhat longer than you estimated, which may be why the building hasn't sold in six months. With a relatively minor adjustment to the repair and improvement estimate and a rather small 10 percent investor discount for my time and effort, I can quickly take this building off your hands and help you avoid any additional holding costs. My offer is summarized below.

Fair Market Value (in fixed-up condition):	$300,000
Repairs and Improvement Costs:	(100,000)
Holding and Misc. Costs:	(10,000)
Investor Discount	
(10 percent off Fair Market Value):	(30,000)
Purchase "As Is" offer price:	$160,000

Purchase "As Is" (subject to thorough inspection within 10 days of acceptance).

Closing within 30 days.

Termite letter required. If not already done, please arrange for it to be provided by Termite and Pest Inc., contact Steve at 123-456-7890.

Warmest regards,

Sonal Patel
(contact information)

Though this property is commercial, once again the cover letter starts on a positive note, points out some of the problems with the building, lets the seller know that the buyer is trying for a win-win situation, lists out the particulars to arrive at the offer price, and reminds the seller that the buyer can close quickly and buy "as is." Again, you hope the offer is solid enough to get the negotiations off to a good start.

7

GOLDEN KEY 6—NEGOTIATE LIKE A CHESS MASTER

"**N**egotiating like a chess master" is the final golden key that will help you to Buy Even Lower, so that you can unlock the door to Regular Riches. However, negotiating like a chess master involves more than just smartly negotiating the purchase of a property to get a good discount. It means negotiating in a manner that builds a positive relationship with the seller and others involved in the process.

By negotiating like a chess master, you greatly improve your odds of buying properties at or below the Maximum Purchase Price. If you don't negotiate this way, you'll probably buy fewer of the properties on which you make offers and, in the process, become frustrated with real estate investing. On the other hand, if you do, everyone (you, the seller, the real estate agent, etc.) will feel good about both the process and the outcome (and even look forward to doing business together again).

Throughout this book, from Jill's success story in Chapter 1, to the postforeclosure examples in Chapter 4 (Golden Key 3), to the cover letter stories in Chapter 6 (Golden Key 5), and more, we've illustrated many of the strategies set forth in this chapter.

EVERYONE SHOULD WIN IN THIS CHESS GAME

Negotiating to buy real estate at a discount is a lot like playing chess. Both are intellectual challenges that require strategy and focus. Both require you to anticipate the other side's next move before you make yours and then adapt appropriately when they make theirs. If you're successful, you win the rights to purchase a property at a good discount.

However, you'll find a big difference between the two. In chess, if you're a chess master like Garry Kasparov or Anatoly Karpov, when you achieve the appropriate outcome, you win and others lose. However, when negotiating to buy real estate, no one should feel like a loser. When you negotiate like a chess master in real estate investing, you're aiming for a win-win outcome. You should feel like a winner because you've just locked in the rights to buy a property on good terms. The seller and agent should feel like winners because they've just locked in the sale of the property on good terms. Achieving a win-win outcome is especially important if you plan to buy more properties from this seller (for example, a financial institution) or through the seller's agent (for example, an REO or corporate relocation agent).

Negotiating with a win-win mentality can also prove valuable with sellers and agents you work with only once. Even if you're making a one-time purchase from a financial institution, individual, or real estate agent, this person can become a reference for you and attest to your credibility and professionalism. Good references can help tremendously when you approach another seller or agent who may regard your offer with some degree of skepticism.

One of the best books we've read on negotiating with a win-win mentality is *The Power of Nice: How to Negotiate so Everyone Wins–Especially You!* by Ronald Shapiro. This book details how Shapiro has successfully used this strategy in the sports world, as a sports agent for many professional athletes.

THE GOLDEN RULE

We try our best to live our personal and business lives by the Golden Rule: treat others the way you would like to be treated.

In our world, this certainly applies to real estate sellers and their agents. We believe in being *honest* with them throughout the negotiations—and we encourage you to do the same. Specifically, don't conjure up problems with the house, neighborhood, or community. Don't exaggerate repair costs, holding costs, and so on, although it's appropriate to build in a reasonable buffer (and sellers should expect this). Don't make up stories or say anything that's untrue. If you do, you run the risk of getting caught in your lie later, plus it's not the right way to treat people. In real estate investing (as in any business and in life), most people prefer to deal with honest people.

It's important to be *fair and reasonable*. If the seller makes a reasonable mistake in the listing and you could profit from it, consider telling the seller so he or she can fix it. We've seen listings and ads with typos or oversights in the buyer's favor regarding prices, items to be left with the property, and so on. However, this doesn't mean you need to buy the property at the "new" increased price. If the seller's agent is slightly late returning the accepted contract to you, consider not penalizing the seller or his or her agent for this. If the seller or agent redrafts a heavily marked-up contract and leaves out a term favorable to the seller, point it out. Remember that the seller and agent are people and people make mistakes from time to time, no matter how careful they are. Being fair and reasonable goes a long way to developing your credibility with sellers and real estate agents.

Treat people with *respect*. No matter how desperate sellers may be to sell their properties, don't make them feel less human. Sellers may be distressed people who've lost their jobs, managers in the REO department under pressure from their bosses to sell the property at a certain price, or real estate agents about to lose a listing if they don't sell fast. Resist any temptation to make these people feel worse. In fact, do your best to boost their feelings of self-worth. If you treat people with respect, regardless of the situation, they'll often remember and appreciate this.

Also, no matter how frustrated you become with sellers or agents, *don't be mean, rude, pushy, or overbearing,* even if they're acting this way. Don't say or do something in the heat of the moment, then have to live with these negative consequences for a long time. By consistently showing respect for others, you'll build credibility with the sellers and their agents—people you may deal with in the future or use as references.

If you feel we're putting too much emphasis on the Golden Rule, consider one of the most basic rules of business: *People often do business with people they like.* Therefore, if you have treated the seller and agent with respect, they're more likely to find a way to make the deal work and will be eager to work with you again. This means more deals and more profits.

Follow the Golden Rule and you'll position yourself to develop good relationships with all the people you meet and do business with. To get the results you're seeking, start and finish with the Golden Rule. It should pay significant dividends, and (just as important) you'll feel even better about your real estate success.

PATIENCE IS A VIRTUE

One of the biggest mistakes real estate investors make during negotiations is not being patient. Those who become impatient run the risk of paying too much for a property. Why is this? Some people are simply impatient.

However, there are often other reasons. By the time the negotiations begin, an investor has invested a lot of time and energy in evaluating a property and making an offer and certainly wants something in return: the property. After spending a lot of time looking at and assessing it, the investor may even have become infatuated with it. Many investors simply get caught up in the heat of the negotiations (like a competition, a negotiation can really get the adrenalin pumping). The bottom line: an impatient investor risks accepting a counteroffer that exceeds the Maximum Purchase Price. This can quickly turn a good investment into a bad one.

> **Tips to Help You Be Patient Throughout the Negotiation Process**
> - Get comfortable with Golden Key 4, calculating the Maximum Purchase Price, and know why you should stop there before making an offer.
> - After making your initial offer, work your way up carefully from the Initial Offer Price to the Maximum Purchase Price.
> - Use your Maximum Purchase Price as a guide for when to stop negotiating.
> - Don't let your emotions get the better of you.
> - If you choose to exceed your Maximum Purchase Price, be sure you're making an intellectual decision (e.g., a few thousand dollars above may help you develop a relationship with a key REO agent or REO manager) and not an emotional one.

In summary, don't get caught up in the amount of time and energy you have invested in the property, how perfect the property would be as an investment, or how exciting the negotiations have become. Instead, keep your head on straight, maintain self-control, and be able to stop negotiating when you hit the Maximum Purchase Price.

Don't be surprised if it takes more than a few months of negotiations to purchase a property. In fact, we've purchased many properties after several months of negotiating. For one property, we negotiated for more than a year. In these cases, we usually negotiated up to the Maximum Purchase Price, then we stuck to our Maximum Purchase Price month after month until the seller finally sold the property to us at this price.

As we've discussed, our favorite investment properties are ugly and awful single-family houses in need of repair and improvement. Because these types of properties need so much work, we ask for a significant discount. Typically, this is more than sellers are initially willing to accept. However, as properties increase their length of time on the market, our offers usually appear more reasonable.

Can months of patient negotiations negatively affect the Maximum Purchase Price? After all, as each month goes by, the estimates for a property's Repair and Improvement Costs and Other Costs can increase. Additionally, your Total Investor Discount can be impacted. Sometimes, even the Fair Market Value of the property will change. For all these variables, we suggest you keep an eye on them. However, usually they will not be impacted enough to change your Maximum Purchase Price in the course of a multimonth negotiation. This is especially true with a seller who you're trying to develop a long-term relationship with (e.g., financial institution, REO agent, etc.). After all, he or she expects you to increase your offer, not decrease it during the course of a negotiation.

Additionally, if major or additional Repair and Improvement Costs become a reality, you should be adequately protected in the real estate purchase contract with the thorough inspection provision. Also, for Other Costs, rarely will these costs vary significantly over several months. However, note that interest rates on loans have been known to spike from time to time (though infrequently), and these can have a material impact on your monthly cash flow if you rent or lease/purchase the property. Finally, for the Total Investor Discount, the Minimum Investor Discount Percentage should not have changed (unless you've changed your investment strategy), the Repair and Improvement Hassle Percentage is protected with the thorough inspection provision, and the Negative Property Attributes Percentage should not have changed.

The only variable that may seem to be materially impacted is the Length of Time on the Market Percentage. After all, if a property has continued to sit on the market, any negative reputation associated with this may have increased and the seller may be even more motivated to give you a big discount upon your return with another offer. However, unless there is a reason to believe that the negative reputation has significantly increased, we usually choose not to prey on the seller's added stress and frustration.

Ultimately, it comes back to the Golden Rule, as we try to build good relationships and win-win situations. We don't believe that reducing our Maximum Purchase Price by 1 to 2 percent every month during the course of a multimonth negotiation is conducive to building a good, long-term relationship with repeat sellers. In addition, we enter every negotiation expecting it to take time (remember, patience is a virtue) so we're usually comfortable that our Maximum Purchase Price will protect our profits for many months to come.

No one knows how long it will take for sellers to come around. However, by making solid offers on properties, not going over your Maximum Purchase Price, and being patient, you'll be able to buy a lot of properties with the appropriate Total Investor Discount. Accordingly, your patience will position you to grow your profits in a positive, consistent, and significant manner.

Remember that patience is a virtue during all the phases of playing the negotiation chess game. During initial counteroffers, *patiently increase your price and adjust your terms* at a rate that makes the seller feel as though you're giving up something yet still preserving as much wiggle room as possible. *Once you hit your Maximum Purchase Price,* stop, then patiently remind the seller of your last offer every month. Remember, in chess, moving your pieces around the board too quickly or letting your emotions get the better of your intellect can lose you the game. Don't let this happen to you when you buy real estate. Negotiate with the patience of a chess master.

COMMUNICATE EFFECTIVELY

Communications are a funny thing. No matter how you communicate, there is no guarantee that the person who receives the communication will understand what you mean. After all, we've all been involved in situations where we've sent or received a note, letter, or e-mail and it's read to mean one thing when it really meant something slightly or significantly different. This can even happen when you communicate orally.

One reason for such confusion with communications is that words, especially when taken with other words, can have different meanings. Further confusion can occur due to preconceived feelings about the sender of the communication (e.g., this is a sly investor, I don't like the way this person operates, etc.). With written communications, emphasis on certain words (boldfaced, italicized, and underlined) and punctuation can also have an unanticipated impact. With oral communications, dialect, voice inflection, tone of voice, and long pauses can also play a role.

For all these reasons, we strongly encourage you to communicate carefully to get your message across as effectively and avoid misunderstandings. For better results, here are some suggestions:

- *Choose your words carefully.* Use words or combinations of words that don't have meanings that can be taken the wrong way. "I love your house" could mean "I've got to have it" or be taken as an insincere compliment. "This house is riddled with problems" could mean a significant discount is needed or taken as an overly aggressive negative comment.
- *Keep it simple.* You've probably heard of the KISS principle. We prefer to "Keep It Short and Simple" rather than "Long and Complex." For example, we try our best to keep our cover letters to one page and straightforward (as described for Golden Key 5).
- *Communicate orally (whenever possible).* Even though the terms of your offer are in the contract and on the cover letter, there is nothing like appreciating a person's voice to

convey the appropriate meaning of words. Additionally, if the receiver of the communication seems to misunderstand it, then the sender can recommunicate immediately to clarify the meaning. Many institutional sellers, such as banks and corporations, won't want to deal directly with you. However, don't miss the opportunity to communicate orally with their real estate agents, who can then reconvey your message better.

- *Communicate face-to-face (when appropriate).* Yes, hearing a person's voice can be very effective. However, seeing their facial expressions and hand gestures when communicating can further help you convey a clear meaning. Additionally, like an oral communication over the phone, you can also recommunicate any misunderstood communication. Though this may be the most effective way to communicate, it is also the hardest because it takes the most time. Both parties have to meet somewhere. Therefore, you may need to encourage the seller or his or her agent a little bit to meet you. Also, be quick to sense when they simply don't want to meet you because your forcefulness can become a negative in the negotiations. Therefore, we suggest you use this tip carefully. Often, your initial offer is an appropriate time to meet face-to-face. Additionally, when you are very close to having a deal, you may want to push to meet.

We believe communicating effectively has played a significant role in our success. The words we use are always chosen carefully, and we take the extra time (which usually isn't much) to make phone calls and meet when appropriate. From what we've been told, many other investors simply don't. This gives us an advantage that we truly believe sets us apart and positions us to consistently Buy Even Lower.

LET THE NEGOTIATIONS BEGIN

Exactly when do the negotiations begin? When the buyer submits the initial offer? When the seller makes the first counteroffer? We believe the negotiations actually begin when the seller puts the property on the market. After all, it's the seller's initial offer to the public. This offer contains an offer price (the Asking Price) and other asking terms, including the condition of the property, the decision to include a real estate commission, seller financing, and so on.

Understanding exactly when negotiations begin may seem like semantics. However, it's important to understand this as you think about buying properties to reach your goals. After all, most expert negotiators say that you're in a better position to negotiate a successful outcome when the other side starts the negotiation.

When you assess the seller's opening offer (the asking terms), you can choose to accept the seller's initial offer and purchase the property with the seller's exact terms (Asking Price, etc.). However, if you want to Buy Even Lower, you will rarely, if ever, do this.

Accordingly, you will almost always make an initial offer with one or more terms that are different than what the seller is asking for. At this point in the negotiation, three things can happen:

1. The seller accepts your initial offer.
2. The seller rejects your initial offer.
3. The seller makes a counteroffer to your initial offer.

Now let's look at what each of these scenario really means.

1. Seller Accepts Your Initial Offer

If the seller accepts your initial offer, then you'll presumably be buying the property on very favorable terms. However, rarely do you want the seller to accept your initial offer. This usually means you could have negotiated a better deal. As with chess, remember your opponent's moves in this game for future games. You want to learn from each negotiation and apply this knowledge to future negotiations. If you enter into another negotiation with this seller, you may choose to set your initial offer a little lower than you would otherwise.

2. Seller Rejects Your Initial Offer

If the seller rejects your initial offer without a counteroffer, this isn't a good sign. The seller is either locked into his or her exact asking terms, including the Asking Price, or doesn't believe your offer is credible or reasonable enough to counter.

Sometimes, it's hard to figure out the reason. It often pays to ask the seller or agent. If the seller isn't flexible on the terms, usually you will want to move on to another property for now while the seller's expectations are high. Remember to be patient.

If the seller rejects your initial offer as a lowball offer, assess the situation. If you're trying to build a relationship with the seller or real estate agent involved, this usually poses a difficult situation. Essentially, your credibility as a reasonable, fair investor is at risk if your Initial Offer Price didn't pass the Red-Face Test.

From time to time, the seller's Asking Price and other asking terms will still make the property a good deal for the investor. In this case, simply resubmit an offer with the exact terms the seller is asking. On the other hand, if you believe the seller is willing to compromise, resubmit an offer with terms somewhere between your initial offer and what the seller's asking. The risk here is that the seller may simply reject your second discounted offer again and your reputation as a fair and reasonable investor may get further tainted in the eyes of the seller and/or real estate agent. Carefully think through submitting a second discounted offer if the seller rejects your initial offer without a counteroffer, especially if you're dealing with a seller or agent you hope to work with in the future. You may even want to put a little time between the offers, such as a week or a month. As with chess, learn from these experiences and apply this knowledge to future negotiations.

3. Seller Makes a Counteroffer to Your Initial Offer

If the seller gives you a counteroffer, this is usually good news. It means the seller viewed your initial offer as credible (your offer passed the Red-Face Test) and you have a chance at getting a good deal on the property.

The only time receiving a seller's counteroffer is bad news is when it's a minor change to the original asking terms. For example, if the seller's counteroffer drops the Asking Price from $200,000 to $199,500, the seller is probably telling you that he or she is firm in the Asking Price and believes the property will sell at very close to this price. In this case, you'd probably be wise to move on to another property (at least for a while). If the property is still listed three months later, the seller may have a different perspective.

If the seller's counteroffer is acceptable to the investor, some may choose to simply buy the property for these terms, especially if they're trying to build a relationship with the seller or agent. On the other hand, we rarely do this without another round of negotiations. The only time we might buy at this phase is when we feel like we may run the risk of really upsetting the seller with another counteroffer, such as with an individual who is emotionally attached to the property.

We have two reasons for believing we don't need to accept the counteroffer at this juncture. First, we have a great deal of confidence in our ability to explain the rationale for our next counteroffer in an appropriate (fair, reasonable, honest) manner. Second, we know more profits usually follow when we continue to negotiate patiently.

THE COUNTEROFFER

There are many ways to handle the counteroffer. You will usually want to submit a counteroffer with reasonably bumped-up terms and explain your rationale behind the changes. For example, increase the purchase price by $1,000 to $5,000. (Our rule of thumb is usually 1 to 3 percent for each round, sticking with round numbers such as $1,000 rather than $850.) You can also adjust terms, such as sharing closing costs (legal fees, finance costs, etc.) or paying part or all of the closing costs yourself. Additionally, you can change the closing date from 60 days to 30 or 45 days so the seller can get his or her money sooner. You can also remove the financing contingency so the seller doesn't have to worry about the deal falling through if you can't secure a loan.

The closing costs tend to be a regularly negotiated item when the buyer asks for all or partial contribution from the seller. Be willing to consider negotiating this term but understand how it could affect the profits of the deal. Remember, closing costs play a role in your Maximum Purchase Price; they can often be 2 to 3 percent of the purchase price. Therefore, if you offer to pay all or some of the closing costs, you need to decrease your Maximum Purchase Price by the same amount. Moving up the closing date and removing the financing contingency can also be powerful negotiation points. However, be careful to make sure you have all your financing ducks in a row ahead of time. You don't want to be stuck with a contract that you can't get the financing to fulfill.

Why is it wise to present your rationale to pay closing costs, move up the closing date, or remove a financing contingency? Because it gives you an opportunity to build additional credibility with the seller and agent, and positively differentiate yourself from other investors. Take this opportunity to remind them you're a top-notch investor who will do what you can to close deals quickly and that you can purchase properties in ways that many others can't.

When presenting your rationale for increasing the purchase price between one offer and a subsequent counteroffer, we often state in the cover letter that we're willing to accept a lower investor discount. In later rounds, you can reduce this discount further. Be careful when you increase the Fair Market Value or lower the repair and improvement and holding costs figures in your cover letter. These numbers are often perceived by sellers as relatively firm and well thought out. Changing these numbers can affect your credibility. Nonetheless, we sometimes adjust these numbers and simply explain that we have reevaluated our figures. For example, we might say that we now think the Fair Market Value that is proposed is reasonable or that we're cautiously optimistic that we can get by with slightly fewer costs.

Fair Market Value

A word of caution about the Fair Market Value: *This is a number that everyone should agree on.* If the seller doesn't agree, include a few comps with your next counteroffer to support the Fair Market Value and maintain your credibility. You can consider raising the Fair Market Value as part of your rationale when the seller and agent make this an issue and they're arguably correct. If you do raise this figure, be careful to maintain your credibility by showing selected comps you used. Make sure you still have room to negotiate so you don't exceed your Maximum Purchase Price.

Always be careful when you tinker with the other terms of your offer. For example, never buy a property without adequate title protection and give yourself plenty of time after negotiations conclude to thoroughly inspect the property.

Also, whether you increase the purchase price or improve other terms in the seller's favor, be aware of the precedent you may be setting. After all, you may work with the same sellers and real estate agents for future purchases. Commit every move they make to memory or document the negotiation steps. Use this information as you set your strategy for future negotiations.

If you know the seller never pays closing costs or gives in-house financing, don't ask for this during future negotiations. Conversely, if the seller always pays closing costs or gives in-house financing, be sure to always ask for these. As with chess, try to track the seller's habits and use this information wisely throughout the negotiation process.

Though some don't, you should anticipate that the sellers and agents you negotiate with will remember every move you make during the negotiations and factor this into their future negotiations with you. For example, if you increase your price $5,000 or offer to pay all the closing costs in your first counteroffer, the seller and their agent may expect you to use the same tactic in negotiations on the next property. Therefore, avoid using the same tactic in each negotiation. As with chess, if you move your pieces the same way in every game, you become predictable and are less likely to be as successful.

By varying the way you negotiate—from the initial offer and cover letter to the counteroffer terms—you'll be viewed as a more sophisticated, experienced investor who pays careful attention to each negotiation. At the same time, while you don't want to be too predictable in your negotiating, there is significant value in being predictable to sellers and agents in some areas. How can that be? Simply put, you'll likely experience more success when the sellers and agents see you do certain things the same way every time. This has more to do with being professional and dependable. For example, follow the Golden Rule, be patient, try to use the same real estate purchase contract, use a consistent format for your cover letter, and respond with counteroffer decisions within 24 to 48 hours. Also, point out all changes and your rationale in the counteroffer cover letters. (Like studying a chessboard, this makes it easier for sellers and agents to see which pieces you're moving in a particular negotiation.)

Finally, just because you have a Maximum Purchase Price in mind *doesn't mean you have to pay that amount every time you buy a property*. In fact, if you use these negotiation strategies, then you will have many situations in which you Buy Even Lower and make even more profits for yourself.

LOOK FOR THE "BONE"

One reason we're successful negotiators is that we're able to find the "bone" for each property. Like a dog's favorite chew toy, the bone is a favorite aspect of our negotiations. The bone is any information a seller or agent can appropriately share to help you negotiate to a successful conclusion (that is, the purchase of the property).

In many cases, it's easy to overlook a bone because it appears to be a simple tidbit of information or seems to have little relevance to the negotiations. However, for the savvy negotiator, having this information—the bone—is pure gold.

Remember that the seller, employees of the seller (such as a bank's REO manager), and real estate agents representing the seller are supposed to have the seller's best interest at heart. Therefore, none of these people should be sharing information that can be detrimental to the seller. However, it's important to understand that, in addition to trying to sell the property for the best terms possible, each of these people has additional goals. This may lead them to share certain appropriate information. For example, a homeowner facing a job transfer has a goal of selling the property before moving. When a seller tells you this, you're getting a bone you can factor into your negotiations. If the seller is a financial institution, it may have a goal to sell a certain number of properties by the end of the month, quarter, or year. If the REO manager or agent shares this bone, you can factor this into your negotiations. Perhaps the REO manager is in a contest to sell a certain number of properties during a certain period; this information can be a nice bone, especially as the deadline approaches.

Consider these examples of finding the bone and using it to negotiate like a chess master.

Bone 1: Reduce the Portfolio Now

Financial institutions such as banks and mortgage companies may have too many foreclosed properties on their books and may be faced with reducing their portfolios quickly. For example, ABC Bank averages 400 properties in its postforeclosure (REO) department's portfolio at any one time. In ABC Bank, the REO manager is Sharon Jacobs and her boss is Richard Singer. ABC Bank has an unusually high number of foreclosures and, subsequently, Ms. Jacobs is carrying more than 1,000 foreclosure properties on her books.

Mr. Singer notices the high number of foreclosures and approaches Ms. Jacobs, advising her that 1,000 foreclosures is far too many for her to have on her books. He gives Ms. Jacobs a directive to reduce the number of postforeclosures to 750 within 30 days, then to 500 within 60 days. In turn, Ms. Jacobs calls the REO agents carrying the listings for these properties and tells them, "We've got to unload properties—now! The asking prices on the entire portfolio are being reduced by 15 percent immediately."

The agents, in turn, generally pick up the phone and call investors they know who might be interested in the properties. They may even call investors who haven't previewed the properties. The REO agent advises the investors of the seller's directive to move the property, notes the price reduction, and asks them to submit a "best and final offer" as soon as possible.

In this situation, the bone is the information regarding the bank's decision to substantially discount its properties and reduce the size of its portfolio. The seller (ABC Bank) wants investors to have this information with the goal of obtaining offers and quickly moving the properties off their books. Accordingly, the REO manager, her boss, and the REO agents simply shared extra information that was in the best interest of the seller.

For this type of bone, all investors may not be treated equally. Investors who have solid reputations as those who regularly close on their contracts (for example, investors who don't back out of contracts due to financing or minor repairs discovered during the inspection) may get the call first. Because they've proven they're easy to work with, they're often the first ones to get these bones. This is why you build rapport and credibility through all negotiations you're involved in. If you've followed the Golden Rule, you're likely to get these bones of information that lead to profits.

With this bone, you clearly have an opportunity to Buy Even Lower than you would have before the call. However, this doesn't guarantee that you'll purchase the property or get a particular discount. As always, carefully consider each step in the negotiations and make your next move prudently. Because the seller wants to sell the property fast, you may not have to increase your next offer significantly. Additionally, if you've reached your Maximum Purchase Price, take this opportunity to resubmit your offer as your "best and final" offer.

Bone 2: End of the Quarter

ABC Bank pays its employees in the REO department a bonus if they move a certain number of properties off their books each quarter. Some employees in the department tend not to focus on this bonus until the last month of the quarter when they realize they may come up short. These managers may be willing to accept extra discounts on properties during this one-month period.

As a savvy investor, you've built a strong relationship with these REO agents. Before the end of every quarter, you ask these managers if they're discounting any of their properties. If they give you this bone, then proceed with the negotiations as in the example above.

Bone 3: They'll Probably Take . . .

You'll be amazed how many times you can receive a valuable answer to the question, "What do you think they'll take?" Ask this question to learn the minimum purchase price the seller will accept.

Sometimes representatives for the sellers (REO agents or the financial institution) know this information and will share it. Other times they don't know but are willing to give you their best guess. Of course, sometimes you can't get this information at all.

We've received numerous tidbits of information from these representatives, especially those with whom we've built strong relationships. These tidbits have proven to be extremely valuable in negotiating the best deal possible on numerous properties. If you get this type of bone, use it to your advantage. This can play a big role in your ability to negotiate like a chess master.

Bone 4: No Owner Financing

Though we often put owner financing into our offer with financial institutions, we've learned that it can actually be a negative hot button. Financial institutions such as banks and mortgage companies are in the business of lending money. Therefore, you'd expect them to try to "kill two birds with one stone" by selling foreclosed properties and generating new loans to the buyers at the same time. However, many banks' foreclosure (REO) departments simply aren't synchronized with their lending departments. Accordingly, owner financing actually adds red tape and angst for the foreclosure or REO employee trying to sell the property. Although having the financial institution give you a loan may seem like a good way to save time and money, this can turn into a bad sticking point, causing the seller not to agree to sell you the property. Therefore, if the financial institution rejects your initial offer or the negotiations are moving slow, ask whether the in-house financing is the problem. If they tell you it is, they just gave you a bone.

Along the same lines, individuals selling their own property who initially seemed open to owner financing actually may get "cold feet" about lending a complete stranger money. Therefore, if you can figure this out, you may be able to work out a negotiation. Investors looking for no-money-down opportunities may experience this situation a lot.

Remember, if the seller doesn't provide owner financing, your finance costs will be higher. Knowing this may help move the negotiations along but be sure to decrease your Maximum Purchase Price to capture the additional expense you will incur if you buy the property.

Bone 5: The Seller Needs to Keep the Sales Price High

Some sellers simply want to sell a property at a certain price. These sellers are willing to throw in other benefits with real value to the investor to achieve their price. Benefits can include closing costs, owner financing, repair money, property furnishings, and more.

If the seller is a financial institution, then the REO manager may have committed the department to sell a certain number of properties for a certain amount of money. For example, the manager may have committed to sell 100 properties for $20,000,000 total. The department must achieve an average sales price of $200,000 per property. At the same time, the manager may have a budget allowing extra benefits to the buyer.

You may also run across this if you're purchasing a house from people who simply don't want to be the "only ones in the neighborhood who sold their property on the cheap" or "weren't smart enough to sell for the same price everyone else is getting." These sellers have put significant psychological pressure on themselves to receive their sales price. But this still leaves the door open for other benefits of the sale from the seller.

How do you find this bone? It usually isn't easy to spot early in the negotiations. However, after a round or two of negotiations, you may find it. With financial institutions, simply say to the employee or the real estate agent, "It seems like we're stuck on the price. Is there anything else we can do?" Sometimes they'll offer to pay full closing costs, even though they had negotiated you down to paying only half. They may also choose to give you the in-house financing that they previously didn't want to. They may even offer to set up a repair escrow account for you, which, in essence, is cash to do your repairs. (Be careful with repair escrow accounts if you receive outside financing; many loans have stringent restrictions on repair escrows.) If they don't throw you a bone, consider asking for one of these.

If you're dealing with individual homeowners, they may be willing to pay all or most of the closing costs to stick to the sales price. Some who were initially resistant about providing owner financing for all or part of the property may now be more open to it, especially when you present the potential return and your creditworthiness. Others may consider leaving furnishings and appliances, even though they initially planned to take these.

Often, other benefits with real value are sitting right under your nose. The key is to know what they look like and how to get them. Keep your eyes open for the bones—they can be extremely valuable in your negotiations. When you find one, remember to increase your Maximum Purchase Price to include it, carefully assess your position in the negotiation, and make your next move accordingly.

OTHER NEGOTIATION STRATEGIES

You can employ a variety of negotiating strategies from time to time. The key is to use the right strategy at the right time. Jill used several of these in Chapter 1 for her successful purchase.

Negotiation Strategy 1: Lay Low

After a round or two of negotiating, you may still have a significant gap between your Maximum Purchase Price (even if you haven't reached it yet), and the seller's current Asking Price. The Lay Low strategy allows you to put some time in between the seller's last counteroffer and your next counteroffer. By doing this, hopefully the seller has not sold the property and will be more open after some additional holding time (and costs) have elapsed to reconsider the seller's last counteroffer.

This strategy is best used when the gap between the potential buyer and seller is more than 10 percent of the Fair Market Value of the property. For example, let's assume the Fair Market Value of a property is $200,000, your Maximum Purchase Price is $150,000, your current offer price is $130,000, and the seller's current Asking Price is $180,000. In this case, $20,000 ($200,000 × 10%) is 10 percent of the Fair Market Value and the gap is $30,000 ($180,000 − $150,000).

If you've only had one round of negotiations, you may choose to wait a week or two, since you're not yet sure how firm the seller is on his or her purchase price. If you've completed two or more rounds and you still have the big gap, you might choose to wait a month or more before your next counteroffer.

You also need to consider where your current offer is in relation to your Maximum Purchase Price. If you've got a lot of room, you may not need to Lay Low yet. However, if you're getting close (such as within 5 percent of your MPP), then the Lay Low strategy may be just what you need to use not to exceed the MPP and still purchase the property at a later date. As the clock continues to tick, it is amazing what an asset time becomes for the buyer.

In Chapter 1, this is one of the strategies Jill used for her successful purchase. Instead of waiting until she reached her MPP to Lay Low, she used this strategy early on in the negotiations to position herself to end up at or below the MPP later in the negotiations. By putting a month in between offers, she could come up $5,000 or less each counteroffer, while the seller came down $10,000 or more each time. Yes, she risked losing the property each time she used this strategy but she also continued to look at other properties (maybe even made some offers), while she negotiated to buy the condo at the appropriate investor price.

When using this strategy don't be surprised or confused when you have gotten the seller to come down on the Asking Price, yet the newspaper or Internet still shows a higher Asking Price. This can occur for several reasons. Sometimes the seller is still truly hoping to get the Asking Price or something close to it. Other times the seller may simply be wanting to use it as a starting place for negotiations with another buyer, so there is some wiggle room to negotiate. It is also possible that the seller or seller's agent has simply forgotten to update one or more advertisements.

Whatever the reason, use this information to your benefit. If the seller is publicly asking too much for the property, he or she is less likely to sell it. Therefore, you may have a better chance of buying it if you negotiate well. On the other hand, this information may reveal that the seller will need even more time to come down to your Maximum Purchase Price. If the seller stops at the higher Asking Price for a while and then reduces it, he or she may be ready to deal.

Keep an eye on this and look for clues from the seller or agent. "I know we've negotiated to this price, but we're still going to try and get more" may mean the seller will need more time. "We just realized why we may not have sold, the newspaper made a mistake." This may be the time to get the deal closed before others see the reduced Asking Price. Whatever the clues, use your judgment to determine your next move.

Using this strategy has been one of the biggest reasons for our success. Yes, we've lost out on our share of properties. However, we've also purchased many properties using it. One of the big reasons for our success with this strategy is that we always like to keep a lot of irons in the fire. We never know which ones will pay off, or how long the negotiation process will last with a particular seller. However, because we continue to look for good properties, make solid offers, and negotiate with the strategies in this chapter, we position ourselves for properties to Buy Even Lower on a consistent basis.

Negotiation Strategy 2: Pick the Season

There are certain times of the year that are more of a buyer's market. In other words, buyers are likely to get better deals during these months of the year. The best times of year to buy properties varies depending on the type of property.

For example, if you're targeting residential properties that usually house families with children, then the buyer's market for these properties are often the fall and winter seasons. One of the reasons for this is that most families with children of school age don't like to move during the school year. Many families simply don't want their children to deal with the trauma of new friends and teachers while school is in session. Therefore, depending on the location, sellers of these types of properties will often tend to see less interest beginning in August or September, with significant drop offs from October to February. Beginning in March, these families often start looking again, as the end of the school year in May or June begins to become imminent.

Another factor tends to be the weather. Regardless of the property type, many people simply don't like to move when it is cold. Therefore, October through March often leads to slower sales in many northern states and December through February in many southern states. Jill leveraged this strategy in Chapter 1.

There are also other factors that might impact your community, such as the rainy season or the hurricane season. You should learn what factors impact your community.

When using this strategy, also remind yourself that if you buy a property during one of these seasons, you now have become a seller or landlord. Therefore, these factors that can positively impact your ability to Buy Even Lower can also negatively impact your ability to sell, rent, or lease/purchase. Accordingly, you may want to factor an extra month or two of costs into your Maximum Purchase Price calculation for these situations.

Also, keep in mind that your negotiations may transcend two or more seasons (especially if you employ the Lay Low strategy).

Therefore, you may want to work harder to close a purchase if the buyer's market is about to change to a seller's market. Additionally, if you use this strategy consistently, the slow season may create significant profit opportunities, as you may encounter sellers who are tired of sitting on their properties and/or simply worn out from the process. Not only may these situations potentially create great Buy Even Lower opportunities, but they could also create excellent selling, renting, or lease/purchasing opportunities as the prime seasons for these are right around the corner. Indeed, during our real estate careers many of our best purchases have been made during the fall and winter seasons.

On a side note, while this tip does not relate specifically to Buying Low, future landlords may want to note that we employ the pick-the-season strategy in the lease/purchasing of all our homes. More specifically, all of our leases are structured to expire in the spring or early summer. Therefore, if we sign up a lease/purchaser in November, we sign a three-and-a-half-year lease/purchase agreement rather than our normal three-year lease.

Negotiation Strategy 3: Name the Closing Date

Some sellers need to sell their property at a certain time. Examples include a financial institution with quarterly quotas, an REO manager who wants to attribute the sale to this month's quota, or homeowners who want to wait until they find and close on another property.

If you have the financial ability to close on a property with flexibility, you may choose to tell the seller that. To have this financial flexibility, you will probably require a large line of credit, enough cash on hand, or simply an arrangement with your lender. With this financial flexibility in your back pocket, consider stating it in your initial offer and cover letter as "buyer can close whenever seller is ready; immediately or several months from now." If possible, ask sellers about their goals before you include this benefit in your offer. By adding this benefit in the contract, you set yourself apart from other offers and may negotiate a better purchase price.

Negotiation Strategy 4: Date Cross-Through

Many investment purchases take several rounds of negotiations (remember, patience is a virtue). Often, it's helpful to remind sellers of the amount of time that has passed during the negotiations—whether it's several days, weeks, months, or more than a year. This reminder can give them an additional appreciation for your offer. After all, the clock has continued to tick, they still haven't sold their property, and they want to sell.

To use the Date Cross-Through strategy, cross through the date of your previous offer on the cover letter and handwrite in the date of your latest counteroffer. When you cross out the previous date, make sure the seller can still read it. Add the new date close to the crossed-out date. This strategy reminds sellers how long they've been trying to sell the property.

We've often use this strategy if we've reached our Maximum Purchase Price without acquiring the property. Simply check in with the seller or seller's agent every month to see if it has been sold. If it hasn't, we resubmit our last contract offer and final cover letter, scratching through the old date and replacing it with the current date.

What do sellers think when cover letters show up again month after month with multiple crossed-out dates? At some point, most sellers must ask themselves if it makes sense to continue to hold the property or accept the offer that keeps coming to their desk every month. Your cover letter showing multiple dates serves as a psychological timeline—a not-so-subtle reminder to sellers that their properties have remained unsold for many months. This is one of the strategies Jill used in Chapter 1 to buy her property, and we've also purchased many properties using this strategy.

Negotiation Strategy 5: Must Accept before Others

As you become more comfortable with real estate investing, you'll probably be looking at many properties over time. Don't be surprised to find yourself considering two or more properties as good investments at the same time. We recommend you buy only one property at a time until you sufficiently build up your experience to handle two or more at the same time. Also, many investors select the best property, make an offer, and see where the negotiations end up. If they don't purchase the property, they move to the next one.

Of course, you run the risk of losing the second property while your focus is on the first one. One way to manage this is by making offers on both properties simultaneously with a contingency. Again, sellers prefer minimal contingencies and they probably won't be thrilled with this one. However, your contingency lasts only 24 to 48 hours and can help push the seller to accept your offer.

Make the contingency provision simple and straightforward, for example: "This offer is contingent on being accepted before any other offers purchaser has made to purchase other real estate in the last 48 hours are accepted." Be sure to point out this contingency in your cover letter.

You accomplish two goals with this contingency. First, you can make multiple offers at the same time, so you don't lose out on good Buy Even Lower opportunities. Second, you let the seller know that you're a serious investor who will buy a property soon. Psychologically, for some sellers, you have now turned this into a minicompetition with some sellers. They need to decide whether to accept your offer—and make a decision faster than the other sellers—to win you as a buyer.

It's possible you could get two sellers who agree to accept your offer at the same time (or believe they have) and may both try to force you to buy their properties. This has never happened to us, but it could. Therefore, we suggest reserving this strategy until you're experienced enough to handle two properties at a time.

Using this strategy on numerous occasions, we've made multiple offers and received fast, accepted offers from time to time. Yes, it works!

Negotiation Strategy 6: Meet You Halfway

It's best to use the Meet-You-Halfway strategy after a few rounds of negotiations. One of our favorite strategies, it works well when the gap between the seller's current offer price and your current offer price is within a reasonable amount.

Be sure to assess whether the midway point between the seller's current offer price and your current offer price is below your Maximum Purchase Price. If so, this is an opportune time to use this strategy.

You'll want to wait for a few rounds of negotiations before using it for three reasons. First, early in the negotiations, the buyer and seller are usually too far apart in price to meet halfway and the midway price may be above your Maximum Purchase Price. Second, the seller may be unwilling to seriously consider this gesture in the early stages of negotiation and you could lose some credibility. Therefore, be careful not to use this strategy too early. Third, after a few rounds of negotiations, the seller should know you are sincere and be prepared to close the negotiation with an agreement to sell the property to you.

To use the Meet-You-Halfway strategy, you may want to add a statement in your cover letter that says: "Because both sides are obviously interested in reaching an agreement on the property, I am willing to meet you halfway. We hope you will take this as a sincere attempt to conclude negotiations and reach an agreement."

An advantage of this strategy is that there are only so many times in the negotiation process that you can claim to be able to accept a lower investor discount or reduce your repair budget buffer. If negotiations go more than two rounds, you will be hard-pressed to find additional reasons to justify your increase in offer price other than simply moving up because you allowed yourself wiggle room. When you ask the seller to Meet You Halfway, you don't have to give any justification. It's simply time to compromise and finish the deal.

Negotiation Strategy 7: Best and Final Offer

This strategy often gets the seller's attention. However, you should save it for your last counteroffer. In other words, you should really mean it.

If you declare an offer is your "best and final" one, then later make another counteroffer, you risk losing credibility with both the seller and agent. This can affect negotiations on the current property and have a lasting, negative impact on your ability to develop a long-term relationship with the seller and agent.

On the other hand, seriously consider using this strategy when you reach your Maximum Purchase Price because it can significantly increase your credibility with the seller and agent. When you make a Best and Final Offer and stick to it, you prove you are sophisticated and experienced. It also sends the message— for this negotiation and future ones—that you carefully think through each round of negotiations. Further, you show that you know when to walk away from a deal—and that you're willing to walk away—when other investors might get caught up in the heat of negotiations or the emotional attachment to the property.

Just because the seller doesn't accept your Best and Final Offer doesn't mean you won't get the property. In fact, we've had several situations in which the seller has come back to us (sometimes several months later after we presented our Best and Final Offer.)

If your final offer isn't accepted and the seller doesn't contact you later, does that mean you can't go back to the seller with another offer? No. However, we suggest you wait a month or so before touching base with the seller or agent again to see if the property is still on the market. If so, simply resubmit your Best and Final Offer. (Be sure to cross off the previous date on the cover letter and add the new date.)

How does it impact your credibility when you've previously told the seller you were submitting your final offer? Most sellers will view your previous offer as the Best and Final Offer for that round of negotiations. In essence, you stuck to your guns, walked away from the negotiations, and let a month or so pass without any contact regarding the property. The sellers usually view your new contract submission as a new negotiation. In fact, many sellers and agents will be pleasantly surprised to hear you're still interested in a property that's been languishing on the market. More important, when you come back with the Best and Final Offer, you haven't changed its financial terms. Your reputation as a sophisticated, experienced investor who knows where to draw the line and keeps your word should remain intact. It may even enhance your credibility!

Jill used this strategy effectively in Chapter 1. We also have used this strategy many times to Buy Even Lower.

Negotiation Strategy 8: Real Estate Agent Reduces Commission

This strategy is listed last because we rarely use it. The agents' commissions provide their livelihood and are regarded as extremely personal. Usually, all agents get for their time and effort is their commission. In fact, some can become testy when you ask for a reduction. The only times we consider asking an agent to reduce his or her commission is when we're sure we won't work with this agent again or when it simply makes too much sense not to ask.

On the other hand, there is nothing wrong with accepting an offer of a reduced commission from an agent. In fact, if you don't, you may insult the agent and hurt your long-term relationship. If agents make this offer, you can assume they've carefully thought it through. They probably concluded that, for all the time, effort, and money they've invested, a reduced commission will still be a reasonable return on their investment. They've probably factored in the additional time, effort, and money they'd have to invest to sell the property to another buyer if you didn't purchase it.

When assessing whether to accept an agent's offer to reduce his or her commission, first determine whether the reduced commission allows you to purchase the property at or below your Maximum Purchase Price. If so, accept the offer. If not, you probably don't want to accept it. Simply follow up with an open, honest conversation with the agent. Thank him or her for the gesture and explain that you can't buy the property on the current terms and still make an appropriate investor profit. A reasonable real estate agent will appreciate this honest discussion and won't hold it against you. You may want to point out that the commission reduction brings the seller's current offer and your offer closer, but you still need a specific monetary adjustment from the seller. This may help nudge the seller to make the necessary, final adjustment to the sales price.

The only time we consider accepting the agent's offer when we're still above the Maximum Purchase Price is if developing a relationship with the agent or seller presents a significant, additional value to our real estate business. In this case, we'd expect to make it up in profits on future Buy Low purchases from this agent.

AFTER NEGOTIATIONS CONCLUDE

Once the negotiations end, you're close to purchasing the property. Often, you'll be the proud owner within 30 to 60 days. However, there are still a few critical stages that the savvy investor should take seriously: *finalizing the contract, conducting a thorough inspection, and preparing for the closing.*

Finalize the Contract

After the negotiations conclude, many buyers and sellers simply sign the final real estate purchase contract and move into the next phase. However, carefully read through the contract before you sign it. Make sure all new and modified provisions are easy to read, have been initialed, and contain the complete and appropriate verbiage. You may even choose to rewrite the contract so it's easier for everyone, especially the closing attorney, to use. This can help you avoid surprises at the closing table.

Also be sure to give your earnest money to the seller or agent. Until you do this, the contract is not legally binding. Make sure you receive an original of the final, fully signed contract. If you have to go to court for any reason, the judge will want to see the original contract, not a copy.

Finally, if you're dealing with financial institutions, they might be slow to execute originals. If they've worked with you on many deals, they may even tell you it's not necessary to have originals executed—that fax copies or simply the exchange of earnest money is fine. If you go along with their requests, be sure you understand the risks. In our experience, after we've purchased several properties from a seller, we do consider accepting faxed copies instead of originals because we don't want to negatively affect the relationship. However, we never feel completely comfortable with this situation and do our best to avoid it.

Conduct a Thorough Inspection

Make sure the thorough-inspection provision is in the real estate purchase contract. While the contract is being finalized, quickly line up an appointment with an inspector. To find a good one, ask for references from other investors, real estate agents, and real estate attorneys. You can also find inspectors in the

phone book and on the Internet. If you have experience with repairs and improvements, the inspector can be a trusted contractor or simply you (unless the contract requires a certified
inspector).

Ask the inspector to conduct the inspection and give a report
as quickly as possible. If you wait until the eighth, ninth, or tenth
day—and you only have ten days to perform the inspection—you
run the risk that the inspector is unable to schedule it or perform
a thorough one. Also, give yourself as many days as possible because you'll need time to understand the inspection report. From
it, you can determine whether any additional repairs are required
and if you'll ask the seller to make these repairs or compensate
you for them.

The inspection report will spell out problems with the
property that you're already aware of. It should provide a full
assessment of these so you'll know if they're severe and more
costly than you'd estimated. If the inspector points out new
problems, quickly obtain additional estimates and analyze their
impact on your profits. Also, you may choose to begin scheduling the appropriate repair people to begin the work after the
closing.

The inspection process helps ensure that you identify and assess all problems, understand repair costs, and line up workers to
make the repairs. It can also provide an opportunity to reopen negotiations and ask for additional discounts to cover unexpected
repairs.

If you're unlikely to deal with the seller or agent again, you
may decide to bring all problems back to the seller. After all, on
the retail market, properties are sold at or close to Fair Market
Value and buyers often come back with a complete list of all problems not previously disclosed to the buyer.

Many states require sellers to use a disclosure form to tell potential buyers about all problems they know about. For these situations, understand that you have extra leverage when bringing
to the seller's attention certain problems such as termite damage,
the need for a new roof, or a furnace that needs to be replaced.

From this point forward, the seller must list this on the disclosure form for all future potential buyers.

On the other hand, if you're developing a long-term relationship with a seller or agent, we suggest you only reopen negotiations when there are *big-surprise* problems. What's a *big surprise?* Any problem with the property that you didn't identify and consider in your offer, and one that's large enough to have a material impact on your profits.

Examples include

- major termite damage,
- major plumbing problem,
- electrical system that needs to be rewired,
- water-damaged support beams that need to be replaced,
- a roof that needs to be replaced rather than patched,
- heating and air-conditioning system that needs to be replaced, and
- all interior walls that need to be painted, not just a few rooms and/or all carpet throughout the property that needs to be replaced, not just cleaned (especially if these had been difficult to determine before the inspection if you first saw the house with the electricity turned off).

When you bring these problems to the seller's attention, the seller may choose not to fix them, further discount the property, or compensate you in any other way. In this case, unless there is still room under your Maximum Purchase Price to cover these extra costs, you may have to walk away from this property.

Keep in mind that for those who want to build long-term relationships (with REO agents, financial institutions, etc.), this probably won't help. For the sake of those relationships, it's important to carefully assess whether the new repair is truly a big surprise. Even if a problem seems like a big surprise to you, the seller or agent may not perceive it as one. Assess its magnitude *from both perspectives* before you make a decision.

When **I**s a **P**roblem **B**ig **E**nough?

How do you determine whether the newly revealed problem is *big enough?* One approach is to apply a threshold, such as 2 percent of the Fair Market Value of the property. After all, you should already have some buffer built into your repair costs for smaller repairs. For example, you're purchasing a house with a Fair Market Value after repairs of $100,000. The inspection report points out the need for a new furnace costing $3,000. Because this amount exceeds your 2 percent threshold, you may consider this a big-surprise problem. If this house simply needs new carpet costing $1,000, this problem may not be big enough to bring back to the seller.

In another example, you're purchasing an office building with a Fair Market Value of $500,000 and discover a big surprise: termites have eaten away the support beams. The repair estimate is $10,000. On the other hand, if the termite report finds that termites have eaten some of the exterior wall and the estimated repair cost is $2,000, this may not be a big enough problem to bring to the seller's attention and reopen negotiations.

Also, put yourself in the shoes of the seller and agent. How would you react if you were them? Will they believe this problem is worth making an issue over after negotiations have closed? Or will they perceive that you are nickel-and-diming them? Often, this decision comes down to your relationship with the seller and agent—how long you've worked with them, your current standing with them, and potential future business with them.

It's also important to determine if this problem should truly be considered a surprise. If you didn't know about the problem, then it's a surprise to you but will the seller and agent perceive it as one?

Is the **P**roblem **R**eally a **S**urprise?

There are two ways to approach whether the problem should be treated as a real surprise. Each approach looks at the surprise from the seller's and agent's perspective. We suggest using both approaches as a check and balance.

Is *the* **P***roblem* **R***eally a* **S***urprise? (continued)*

First, refer to all of your cover letters from the negotiations. If you never mentioned the big-surprise problem in any of your cover letters, then most likely they'll more readily understand that you didn't factor the problem into your offer. If you did refer to this problem in your cover letters, you may need to assess whether you'll be able to reasonably explain that the problem is significantly larger than you anticipated.

Second, put yourself in their shoes. If you were the seller and agent, would you consider this to be a real surprise? Should the investor (you) have seen or known about this issue? For example, the need to replace old carpeting, flooring, furnaces and air-conditioning units are problems that investors should reasonably anticipate. After all, even if the lights are off, the seller and agent may assume that an experienced, sophisticated investor would carefully assess the property with a flashlight before making any offer.

Before taking action, determine whether you really need to raise this issue. Did you build enough buffer into your repair costs or is there still room under your Maximum Purchase Price to absorb the cost to repair this big-surprise problem? If your answer is yes, then seriously reconsider bringing this surprise problem back to the seller. After all, sellers don't appreciate it when buyers come back asking for more after the negotiations are complete. Again, this probably won't help you in building a relationship with either the seller or the agent. Therefore, when you deal with potential long-term sources of properties, do everything you can to avoid classifying a problem as a real surprise.

When bringing a big-surprise problem back to the seller, consider how you should handle reopening negotiations. We suggest you kick it off with a verbal communication. This way you can immediately sense whether the agent or seller understands. If they act irritated, you can then quickly verbally respond to try and maintain the relationship. You will then usually follow up with a summary of the big-surprise problem in writing.

Reopening the negotiation process will be easier if you've practiced the Golden Rule during your negotiations with the seller. Consider if he or she likes and trusts you, even if negotiations dragged on, which is sometimes unavoidable. Before reopening the negotiation, obtain a few estimates in writing from qualified contractors. When you call the seller, *explain that it's your policy to not resubmit an offer after inspection unless the discovered problem is significant and a real surprise.* Further, explain that you don't intend to benefit from this issue, that you want the price adjusted only by the cost to repair the problem. Finally, say that you have two estimates and will take the lower of the two as the necessary adjusted price. Offer to fax the seller a copy of the estimates and the inspection report detailing the problem.

Prepare for the Closing

During the closing, the property is legally transferred from the seller to the buyer. Laws and procedures for the closings vary from state to state. In some states, the closings are administered by real estate attorneys. In others, title companies perform the closings.

Begin preparing for the closing immediately after the real estate purchase contract is negotiated and signed. You want to ensure the closing goes smoothly and you want to prepare for the postclosing period (getting contractors started, marketing the property, etc.). After all, time is money. If you don't start on these tasks until after the closing, your profits will be negatively impacted.

Before the inspection. You'll have multiple minor tasks to perform before the inspection and after it (particularly if the inspection reveals a big surprise and you need to reopen negotiations). Because you don't know what the thorough inspection will turn up, don't spend a lot of time and money preparing for the closing until this phase is over.

After the contract is signed, contact your lender to begin the loan process. Ask the lender's representatives to start doing everything they can without an application fee. Though most of the work will require the application fee, they may be able to complete certain paperwork to start the ball rolling. Most lenders won't assess a fee in the event that the contract is canceled due to an issue discovered during the inspection. If you're concerned about this cost in case you need to back out of the contract, it may be prudent to discuss this possibility in advance with your lender. If you're getting owner financing, be sure to confirm this process in the beginning. Also, start lining up repair people and an insurance policy. However, don't pay any money until after the inspection and any ensuing negotiations are complete.

After the inspection. After the inspection and any ensuing negotiations over problems are complete, start doing the major tasks needed to prepare for the closing. Your goal is to make sure the closing goes smoothly and get ready for postclosing.

Meet with your *lender* representatives, give them your application fee, sign the paperwork, and start moving the loan approval process full-speed ahead. Don't be surprised if the loan process isn't complete until just days before (or the same day of) the closing. Many mortgage companies work toward deadlines (the closing dates) instead of completing the paperwork as quickly as possible. This is extremely frustrating but is a function of the industry. Once you start the process, check with your lender to ensure the appraisal is completed on a timely basis. You may want to check with your lender weekly to make sure your loan is on track.

Make sure the *closing attorney* or *title company* receives a copy of the contract—the sooner the better. Depending on your lender, you may get to select the closing attorney or title company. This professional needs adequate time to perform a title search and obtain the seller's loan payoff information, property tax information, verification letter of dues paid to the homeowners' association, and much more. Also, tell the closing attorney or title company if you want title insurance, which we recommend. It should only cost you a few dollars for every thousand dollars of the purchase price. As with lenders, closing attorneys and title companies also work toward deadlines too. Check with them several weeks before closing to make sure there are no title problems.

Request to review the settlement agreement (closing statement) 24 to 48 hours before the closing date. The settlement agreement you'll receive breaks down all the financials of the transaction. It tells you how much money you'll need to bring to the closing, usually in the form of a cashier's check. On it, there may be many adjustments to the contract purchase price, such as loan finance costs, unpaid taxes, insurance, and real estate agent commissions. Don't be surprised to find errors when you review the settlement agreement. In our experience, it's a lot easier to find and correct these errors 24 to 48 hours in advance than at the closing table.

If the property you're purchasing needs *repairs and improvements,* put a plan in place so the work can begin as soon as possible after closing. Again, time is money, so determine before the closing whether items need to be repaired or replaced, obtain estimates, and line up contractors to begin immediately after closing.

Contact your *insurance company* and set up an insurance policy to be in force the day of the closing. Decide on the amount of the deductible and coverage, and other variables. You may want to talk to other investors or a real estate attorney to decide the appropriate levels for this property.

Contact all the *utility companies* in advance. Arrange to have the gas, electrical, and water service begin the day after closing so contractors can start their work.

If the repairs and improvements are relatively minor, consider scheduling your *advertisement* to sell, rent, or lease/purchase the property to start the day of or day after the closing. You can immediately begin to collect prospects' names and phone numbers and schedule people to view the property. Also, order a professional-looking For Sale, For Rent, or For Lease/Purchase *sign* to place in front of the property as soon as it's legally yours.

Finally, if you're purchasing your first investment property, consider setting up some *basics* for your real estate investing business. For example, you may want to activate a personal liability policy and set up a corporate entity to protect you above and beyond the insurance policy on the property. You may also want to have a voice-mail number for prospects to call so they don't call you at home or work at all hours of the day or night (and don't keep calling you on an old ad after the property has been sold, rented, or lease/purchased).

THE CLOSING

At the closing, you will sign a lot of papers and give the closing attorney or title company your money (as set forth on the settlement agreement). You'll also probably need to bring a photo ID and show proof of insurance. During the closing, the seller fulfills his or her main obligation—signing over the property to you.

After the closing is over, *congratulate yourself*. Hopefully, you've done everything you set out to do with the particular investment property.

We hope you've been able to Buy Even Lower than you would have if you had not read this book and, even more significantly, Buy Even Lower than most other investors.

8

THE GOLDEN KEY RING—BRINGING ALL THE KEYS TOGETHER

We've tried to cover a lot of ground in this book in a complete, comprehensive, yet concise and readable way—and we hope we've succeeded. To make sure you're ready to get going, we will end with a summary of the Six Golden Keys all laid out in a key ring that brings all of this together.

GOLDEN KEY 1: DETERMINE YOUR MINIMUM INVESTOR DISCOUNT

Select a real estate investment strategy that fits your goals and personal situation. Once you choose the investment strategy that's right for you, apply the appropriate Minimum Investor Discount Percentage to each purchase. Again, the MID Percentages tend to fall into these ranges:

- Buy and Hold is 5 to 10 percent.
- Buy and Lease/Purchase is 10 to 20 percent.
- Buy and Flip is 20 to 30 percent or more.

Once you have your investment strategy and MID% range, then decide how wide a net you want to cast for your target properties. Remember, the higher the MID% you require, the fewer properties you will probably be able to purchase and the harder you will have to work to find them.

Again, we use the Buy and Lease/Purchase investment strategy, as detailed in our book *Buy Low, Rent Smart, Sell High,* and usually employ a MID% of 10 percent. The profits we miss out on by choosing the lower end of the range, we more than make up for with the other five profit sources specific to the Buy Low, Rent Smart, Sell High investment model. Additionally, by casting as wide a net as possible for this strategy, we have more time to find more properties and enjoy our Regular Riches.

🔑 GOLDEN KEY 2: KNOW WHAT GOOD PROPERTIES LOOK LIKE

Determine the type of properties that best suit your real estate investment strategy. Options include developed, undeveloped, residential, commercial, single-family houses, condominiums, town homes, apartments, and more. Once you know what good properties look like, you'll be ready to pounce on Buy Even Lower opportunities that meet your criteria.

We prefer investing in single-family houses in middle-income communities. Houses that have a minimum of three bedrooms and two bathrooms work best for our Buy and Lease/Purchase strategy. We especially like "ugly and awful" properties—houses that need significant cleanup, repairs, or improvements, and have negative attributes (for example, located on a busy street or on a nonstandard lot). Using the Buy and Lease/Purchase strategy for these types of properties has offered us terrific profit-making opportunities.

GOLDEN KEY 3: FIND GOOD PROPERTIES

Select one or two ways to find good discount real estate. Ten common methods include preforeclosures, foreclosure sales, postforeclosures, purchasing from distressed sellers, real estate auctions, tax liens and deeds, pounding the pavement, corporate relocations, estate sales, and bulk institutional buying. The key is selecting the methods that best fit your time, money, and personality—and get good at working with them.

Of these choices, we prefer to find postforeclosure properties that meet our criteria and recommend you try it out for yourself. Not only do postforeclosures offer a large pool of properties, but as an investor, you'll deal with financial institutions rather than owner-occupants who are emotionally attached to their homes. The postforeclosure purchase process provides enough time to thoroughly examine properties and usually takes less time than other options. Additionally, with this method, you're building relationships with real estate professionals (REO managers in financial institutions and REO real estate agents)—relationships that can help you find great deals on properties without spending much time looking.

GOLDEN KEY 4: CALCULATE MAXIMUM PURCHASE PRICES

When you master this key, you learn to systematically calculate the maximum price you should pay for a property to make it a good investment—a critical component if you want to consistently Buy Even Lower.

Practice the method outlined for Golden Key 4 to calculate your Maximum Purchase Price and discipline yourself to use it with every property you consider purchasing. The Maximum Purchase Price provides an objective amount—your ceiling price—that guides you through negotiations and auction bids to purchase properties that will give you a healthy profit.

Again, the Maximum Purchase Price (MPP) formula is the property's Fair Market Value (FMV) minus Repair and Improvement Costs (R&I) minus Other Costs (OC) minus the Total Investor Discount (TID), or MPP = FMV – R&I – OC – TID.

Other Costs include Legal Costs (LEG), Finance Costs (FIN), Taxes and Insurance Costs (T&I), Mortgage Payment Costs (MORT), Utility Costs (UC), Marketing Costs (MARK), Real Estate Agent Costs (REA), and Miscellaneous Costs (MISC), or OC = LEG + FIN + T&I + MORT + UC + MARK + REA + MISC.

The Total Investor Discount (TID) is the Total Investor Discount Percentage (TID%) multiplied by the Fair Market Value (FMV). The Total Investor Discount Percentage (TID%) is made up of the Minimum Investor Discount Percentage (MID%), the Repairs and Improvement Hassle Percentage (RIH%), the Negative Property Attributes Percentage (NPA%), and the Length of Time on the Market Percentage (LTM%), or TID% = MID% + RIH% + NPA% + LTM%.

GOLDEN KEY 5: MAKE SOLID OFFERS

Presenting a solid offer to the seller gets negotiations off to a good start and best positions you to purchase the property at or below your Maximum Purchase Price. If you use an auction to find good properties, this Golden Key helps you determine your initial bid. The three key elements of a solid offer when negotiating are your Initial Offer Price, the real estate purchase contract, and your cover letter.

Again, the Initial Offer Price is determined by selecting an appropriate Wiggle-Room Discount, usually between 5 and 25 percent, and taking this off the Maximum Purchase Price. Make sure your Initial Offer Price passes the Red-Face Test—that is, it should be an appropriate amount that will be taken seriously by the seller and start the negotiation process. Your offer should be made in writing in the form of a legally binding real estate purchase contract. Finally, your cover letter presents your offer in a clear, concise, and professional format, helping ensure the seller perceives your offer as fair and reasonable—solid.

GOLDEN KEY 6: NEGOTIATE LIKE A CHESS MASTER

Strategically negotiate your property purchase to a successful outcome. Like chess, you want each move during the negotiations to position you to "win" the property at or below your Maximum Purchase Price. However, unlike chess, you make each move with the intention of completing the purchasing process with the seller and agent feeling like winners, too. When that's in place, your negotiation is more likely to be successful. And if you're dealing with financial institutions or key real estate agents through respectful negotiations, you'll gain credibility and possibly leads on additional properties to purchase. We suggest you follow the Golden Rule: treat others the way you would like to be treated.

In the heat of the negotiation, exercise patience and don't get caught up in the excitement. Always try to communicate effectively. You may also choose to apply a variety of negotiation strategies, such as Looking for the Bone, Laying Low, Picking the Season, Naming the Closing Date, Crossing Through the Date on the Cover Letter, Meeting the Seller Halfway, and Submitting your Best and Final Offer.

USE THE GOLDEN KEYS WITH CARE

Now that you've read this book, you're probably geared up to buy investment real estate at a discount. Careful, though; this book can be just like having a new, turbo-powered car. When you jump into a brand-new, high-performance car, you don't go full throttle your first time out. In much the same way, get a good feel for each Golden Key and how to Buy Even Lower before you rush out to buy properties. In fact, if you're an inexperienced investor, you may only want to buy one or two properties a year for the first few years.

After all, Buying Even Lower is not a get-rich quick scheme. *It's a consistent method to buy discount real estate and position yourself for long-term, sustainable profits.* Use this book appropriately and pace yourself. For more help in bringing the Golden Keys together, visit our Web site at *www.RegularRiches.com,* where you'll find additional educational materials and a schedule of our seminars. It's also a convenient place to ask us your real estate investing questions or simply stay in touch with us.

We sincerely wish you the best in achieving Regular Riches through your real estate investment ventures. Good luck!

SAMPLE REAL ESTATE PURCHASE CONTRACT

*Free, editable soft copy available at *www.RegularRiches.com/Contract*

A. PURCHASE AND SALE. The undersigned purchaser agrees to buy, and the undersigned seller agrees to sell all that tract of land, with such improvements as are located thereon, described as follows: The house known as

_____ according

to the present system of numbering. Together with all lighting fixtures attached thereto, all electrical, mechanical, plumbing, air-conditioning, and any other systems or fixtures as are attached thereto; all television antennas and mailboxes; and all plants, trees, and shrubbery now a part of the property. The full legal description of said property is the same as is recorded with the clerk of the superior court of the county in which the property is located and is made a part of this agreement by reference.

B. PURCHASE PRICE AND METHOD OF PAYMENT.

The purchase price of the property shall be: _____ dollars. Purchase is contingent on purchaser obtaining an investor loan at __% down payment with an interest rate not to exceed _____% on a _____-year loan.

C. EARNEST MONEY. Purchaser has paid to the undersigned

seller, _____ ($), receipt whereof is hereby acknowledged as earnest money, and is to be applied as part of payment of purchase price of said property at the time of closing. Purchaser and seller agree that the seller shall deposit earnest money in the seller's account by the third banking day following acceptance of this agreement by all parties; all parties have agreed that said escrow/trust account will be an interest-bearing account, with interest also applied to purchase price at time of closing. The parties to this contract understand and acknowledge that disbursement of earnest moneys held by escrow agent can occur only at closing; upon written agreement signed by all parties having an interest in the funds; upon court order; or upon failure of loan approval; or as otherwise set out herein. This contract is voidable at seller's option if the earnest money check is not paid when presented to the drawee bank.

D. WARRANTY OF TITLE. Seller warrants that he or she pres-

ently has title to said property, and at time of closing, he or she agrees to convey good and marketable title to said property to purchaser by general warranty deed subject only to

(1) zoning ordinances effecting said property, (2) general utility easements of record serving said property, (3) subdivision restrictions of record, and (4) leases, other easements, other restrictions, and encumbrances specified in this contract.

E. **TITLE EXAMINATION.** The purchaser shall have a reasonable time after acceptance of this contract to examine the title and furnish seller with a written statement of objections affecting the marketability of said title. Seller shall have a reasonable time, after receipt of such objections to satisfy all valid objections and if seller fails to satisfy such valid objections within a reasonable time, then at the option of the purchaser, evidenced by written notice to seller, this contract shall be null and void. Marketable title as used herein shall mean title which a title insurance company licensed to do business in the state of _____

will insure at its regular rates, subject only to standard exceptions unless otherwise specified herein.

F. **DESCRIPTION OF PREMISES.** Seller warrants that at time of closing the premises will be in the same condition as it is on the date that this contract is signed by the seller, normal wear and tear excepted. However, should the premises be destroyed or substantially damaged before time of closing, then at the election of the purchaser: (a) the contract may be canceled, or (b) the purchaser may consummate the contract and receive such insurance as is paid on the claim of loss. This election is to be exercised within 10 days after the purchaser has been notified in writing by seller of the amount of the insurance proceeds, if any, seller will receive on the claim of loss. If purchaser hasn't been so notified within 45 days, subsequent to the occurrence of such damage or destruction, purchaser may, at its option, cancel the contract.

G. **RESPONSIBILITY TO COOPERATE.** Seller and purchaser agree that such documents as may be necessary to carry out the terms of this contract shall be produced, executed, and/or delivered by such parties at time required to fulfill the terms and conditions of this agreement.

SPECIAL STIPULATIONS

H. **REAL ESTATE TAXES.** Real estate taxes on said property for the calendar year in which the sale is closed shall be prorated as of the date of closing.

I. **STATE TRANSFER TAX.** Seller shall pay state of _____ property transfer tax.

J. **CLOSING DATE AND COSTS.** Sale shall be closed on or before _____ at such time, date, and location specified by seller. Seller shall pay all closing costs in connection with the sale of subject property to purchaser.

K. **UTILITY BILL PRORATED.** Seller and purchaser agree to prorate between themselves, as of the date of closing, any and all utility bills rendered subsequent to closing which include service for any period of time the property was owned by the seller or any prior owner.

L. **WOOD INFESTATION REPORT.** At time of closing seller shall provide purchaser with a wood-destroying infestation report, in the current form officially approved by _____ structural pest control commission, from a properly licensed pest control company stating that the main dwelling has been inspected and found to be free of visible infestation and structural damage caused by termites and other wood-destroying organisms or that if such infestation or structural damage existed it has been corrected. The inspection referred to in such report shall have been made within 30 days prior to closing. The inspection and termite letter is to be provided by _____.

M. **SURVIVAL OF TERMS OF CONTRACT.** Any condition or stipulation of the contract not fulfilled at time of closing shall survive the closing, execution, and delivery of the warranty deed until such time as said conditions or stipulations are fulfilled. [The closing attorney is directed to transfer this paragraph to the closing statement.]

N. **SEWER/SEPTIC TANK.** Seller warrants that the main dwelling on the above described property is served by:

A PUBLIC SEWER_____ OR

A SEPTIC TANK_____

(PURCHASER) (SELLER)

O. WALK-THROUGH AND INSPECTION. Purchaser has the right to walk through the property and to have an inspection of the premises made by a qualified building inspector within 10 business days of acceptance of this contract. Expense of the inspection shall be paid by the purchaser. Should purchaser present to seller within this 10-day period a report citing any deficiencies in the property found during the walk-through or inspection, seller, at his or her option, may elect to correct said deficiencies, request purchaser to accept "as is," or allow purchaser to declare contract null and void. Seller shall have 48 hours to decide which repairs, if any, are to be made. Purchaser shall have 48 hours after notice from seller to accept seller's offer of repairs or declare contract null and void.

This instrument shall be regarded as an offer by the purchaser or seller who first signs to the other and is open for acceptance by the other until _____ o'clock p.m. on the _____ day of _____ by which time written acceptance of such offer must have been actually received by _____. Acceptance can be communicated this week to _____ at:

FAX: _____

PHONE: _____

THE ABOVE PROPOSITION IS HEREBY ACCEPTED, _____ O'CLOCK _____ M., THIS _____ DAY OF _____, ____

_____

PURCHASER, HEIRS, AND/OR ASSIGNS

_____

PURCHASER ADDRESS

_____

SELLER

_____

SELLER ADDRESS

patience, 196–99
real estate agent reduces commission, 222–23
seasonal picks, 216–17
seller accepts initial offer, 202–3
seller makes counteroffer, 204
seller rejects initial offer, 203–4
win-win mentality, 194
Networking, 79

O

OC. *See* Other Costs
Offer, solid. *See* Solid offer
Office building, neglected, 152–54
    cover letter, 189–91
Option money, 19–20
Other Costs (OC), 7, 120, 132–37, 145, 147
Outdated house, 65–66
Outside community investing, 49
Owner financing, no, 211–12

P

Patience, 109–10, 196–99
Perfect house, 154–57
Personal situation, 16
    cash and credit, 26–29
    role of, 20–21
    stress and headaches, 23–26
    time and effort, 21–23
Personality, cover letter, 181
Portfolio
    diversity, 42
    reduction, 209–10
Postforeclosures, 5, 6, 76–77, 95
    bulk institutional purchasing, 98
    call lender, 77–78
    finding good properties, 102, 106
    initial offer, 162
    introduce as investor, 78–81
    Maximum Purchase Price, 150
Potential investment property form, houses, 103–4
Power of Nice, The, 194
Preforeclosures, 71–73, 74
Premises
    condition, 172
    description, 241–42
Price, 118–19
Prime rate, 27

Private mortgage insurance (PMI), 169
Problem property, 57–60
Problems, big-surprise, 227–29
Profit by Investing in Real Estate Tax Liens, 89
Profit from Your Vacation Home Dream, 54
Property
    apartments, 44–45
    appearance, 5, 35–36, 67–69
    condominiums, 44–45
    developed versus undeveloped, 36–39
    development, 37–38
    features, 49–51
    fixer uppers, 55–56, 57
    high income, 45–48
    houses, 44–45
    low income, 45–48
    middle income, 45–48
    mint condition, 55–56
    problem, 57–60
    residential versus commercial, 39–42
    rural, 48–49
    single-family versus multifamily, 42–44
    suburban, 48–49
    urban, 48–49
Purchase contract. *See* Real estate purchase contract
Purchase price, method of payment, 168–69
Purchase and sale of property, 167–68

R

R&I. *See* Repairs and Improvement Costs
Railroad tracks house, 63–64
Real Estate Agent Costs (REA), 133, 136
Real estate auctions, 74–76, 82–86
Real estate companies, finding REO agents, 108
Real estate investment, xi–xiv, 11–12
Real estate owned (REO), 162
    department, 77–79, 98–99
    properties, 95, 102, 104–5
REO manager/agent
    cover letter and, 184
    developing relationships with, 110–12
    finding good, 107–9
    looking for bone, 208–9
    maintaining credibility with, 112–15
    negotiation and, 194, 226
    patience with, 109–10, 197–98
    working with, 104–5